Boomerville

Musings on a Generation that Refuses
To Go Quietly

Rosa Harris

Manor House

Library and Archives Canada Cataloguing in Publication

Harris, Rosa, author
  Boomerville : musings on a generation that refuses to
go quietly / Rosa
Harris.

ISBN 978-1-988058-01-6 (bound).

--ISBN 978-1-988058-00-9 (paperback)

1. Baby boom generation. I. Title.

HQ1059.4.H365 2015
305.244   C2015-906076-1

Copyright: Rosa Harris and Manor House Publishing Inc.

Special thanks to photographer Denton Pendergast for back
cover photography

Cover design/realization Donovan Davie: 519-501-2375
Front Cover Art: 'Baby-Boomer Couple in Love Holding
Hands' courtesy Shutterstock / D. J. McGee

We acknowledge the financial support of the Government of
Canada through the Canada Book Fund (CBF) for this title.

First Edition. 240 pages. All rights reserved.
Published October 15, 2015
Manor House Publishing Inc.
www.manor-house.biz (905) 648-2193

To my beloved children, Theodore and Benjamin,
Millennials, who are making their mark,
and doing me proud

Table of Contents

5

"**Rosa Harris** has assembled a series of very thought-provoking apercus of her times and generation. They are all from different angles and none is ponderous or over-long. The result is a very pleasing, very easy, and often poignant, read."
– **Conrad Black**

"**Rosa Harris**, award-winning journalist, editor, talk show host, journalism professor, has crafted a collection of insightful, humorous and touching essays on the baby boomer generation that will leave you smiling, laughing and reminiscing on the times of your life. Baby boomers will see themselves in many of Rosa's musings on the most amazing generation ever!"
– **Michael B Davie**, author, *Why Everybody Hates Toronto*

Foreword

I've known Rosa Harris for 25 years, starting when she worked at a city magazine in Montreal. It was in the final few months before *Generation X* was published and there was no awareness in the culture that something, anything, might want to cleave away from the baby boomer's stranglehold on all things generational.

The thing that annoyed me more than anything was people telling me, "Oh, but you must remember the JFK assassination." Ugh. No! I don't! Stop telling me I do! I don't!

It was actually the non-existent JFK assassination memory that drove me to create *X*. Here it is, 25 years later, after having slaved away to create my own generation and in the *New York Times* I'm still technically considered a baby boomer. It's never going to end.

Enter Rosa. She's one of the few boomers who is fully aware of just how annoying and self-absorbed her generation really is. She knows the one critical distinction between boomers and everyone who came after: The boomer generation is the only one that unselfconsciously uses the pronoun 'we' when describing itself; X, Y and beyond flee the room the moment someone says 'we.'

Now we have Millennials. *Time* magazine did a cover story on them and the title was almost word-for-word identical to the *Gen X* story it did in the early 1990s... "Who are they???? Adrift. Feeling lost. Self-absorbed. Blah, blah, blah."

I think there's something genetic built into our species that makes us want to demonize anyone who's born a few years behind or ahead of us. That tendency is unlikely to go away.

When people read Rosa's book in 200 years I wonder what they'll think of boomers and their Borg-like sense of unity. By then people will probably be created in batches in a laboratory — which is, in some ways, quite similar to the protected machine-like situation that facilitated the creation of boomers in the first place. So I guess nothing ever changes.

Rosa, at least, is fully aware of the historical forces that had to align to create the most self-absorbed and narcissistic birth cohort in the history of our planet, yet she can really tap into this awareness to create something sensitive and smile-inducing.

I think you'll enjoy this book.

– **Douglas Coupland**, author, *Generation X*

INTRODUCTION

1 Twist and Shout

"Let's face the music and dance."
—from the 1936 Irving Berlin song of the same name

The crowd on this Saturday night is just raucous enough to prove they're in the moment. Most people here are pushing 50. Others are feeling 50 push back.

A rough guess says about 100 movers and shakers – I mean that literally – are making the scene happen as a hot band ups the ante on the amps. If this motley crew's mean age truly is half a century, we're talking 5,000 years of collective experience. All of us have faced a little music. And we're dancing, Mr. Berlin. You bet we're dancing.

The setting is a downtown dive that has been pre-enjoyed by many generations past.

Most of this generation's regulars have checked in. Tonight, though, we're missing the city's consummate blues hound, big Charlie. His knowledge of riffs and licks – of harp players and horn dogs-is legendary.

Charlie generally holds court facing the music at the head of a long table set up just for him. He's affable, warm and totally unthreatening. Still, a person thinks twice before taking up a seat by his side. There's a tacit honour in joining him. You feel you have to be asked.

Heidi, the server with the eagle eye, is scooping up empties and returning with refills. As she slaloms through tables, she's bopping, her tray of drinks boogying precariously along with her. She stops to exchange a joke with someone, laughter erupting all around.

Up on the dance floor, Alexa is cutting a rug with the precision of a surgeon. She and one of her many dance partners sway so effortlessly and with such grace, they make it look easy. It isn't. The rest of us are flailing our arms about as though we're stuck in a 1960s light show. Maybe we are, but who cares? Everyone's watching, but no one is self-conscious.

Tonight's sultans of swing are letting loose on the tiny stage, doing righteous justice to 12-bar blues. The house band wails and when the group tackles a Jimmy Reed number, your nerve endings tingle and your blood becomes fizzy.

The bass player, sporting his signature porkpie hat, probably surpasses the venue's mean age by about a dozen years. He plays with authority – as if he's been around the block and knows a thing or two about where the best joints are.

But the guitarist is a whippersnapper – and the way he channels B.B. King or Muddy Waters is downright eerie. He wields his axe with far too much angst for a kid.

Apart from their age, demographically the crowd is mixed. Sitting in one corner with his regular lady is a wizened

Saturday-night cowboy wearing boots with toes so pointed they could puncture a balloon. His Stetson is tilted just so.

Over at one end of the bar, a guy in a ball cap and a blazer is making eyes at a slick, young woman whose makeup is perfect.

At another table, a gaggle of women is giggling and pointing at a young hunk. He appears to take no notice of them at all, but I catch him looking them over after they've turned away.

The dive is a favourite of the blues crowd, but it's just one of many spots that offer rock-concert quality live shows in the gracious city where I live.

The price of admission is free or a pittance and the events seem designed for geezers like us: Often they start early, so we can crawl back to bed at a decent hour to rest our bones after shaking our booties like it's 1969.

It's a terrible cliché to say 60 is the new 40. I don't buy it at any rate. To paraphrase a friend, I think 60 is the old 60-and that's a good thing.

This may be one of the most carefree periods of our lives. The career is winding down, the kids are grown, the future is finally ours. We didn't have that 20 years ago. We have it now.

And judging from the gang at the Upper Deck, we're making the most of it. Are we having fun yet? Is that a question?

Part 1: DOES THIS DRESS MAKE ME LOOK FAT?

2 The Appearance of lines and wrinkles

"As soon as you Botox your smile lines away, you lose part of your identity."

— British reality TV star Nigel Barker (b: 1972)

If ever there were a morning for one of those swank new facial fillers, surely this was it. The mirror was reflecting the cruel and unusual punishment an intensely lived life can exact on a face over a 60-year-plus span.

That wrinkle? Probably popped out the time we sat in the waiting room, pacing, as our two-year-old son's hernia operation went on for an hour longer than it was supposed to. The surgeon finally appeared, looking unduly somber, mouthing words no one wants to hear under the circumstances. "There's been a slight hitch," he said. The hitch was minor, as it turned out, but the furrow in the brow remains, a testament to parenthood at its most anxious.

That laugh line? Could be the result of the moment our eldest, a toddler at the time, spontaneously took to the stage during a theatre screening of a Sesame Street movie and did his patented Grover imitation for the assembled audience, with a 10-foot-tall Big Bird as his backdrop. Giddy tears poured down my face as I clutched my gut: they found their way into newly forming crevices at the corners of my eyes – crevices that have since settled in for the duration.

That charming crease on the cheek? That might be from the time the same kid, then 17, was supposed to call in from a party taking place out of town. Minutes, then hours, dragged before the call finally came through. The boy came home intact, eventually. The face of his mother was not so lucky. It seemed to have aged instantly.

The siren lure of Botox et al. Just a simple injection among friends at today's version of the Tupperware Party. That's all it would take to lessen the creeping spectre of mortality written all over the face in the mirror. No surgery, no telltale scars. And despite its relationship to deadly botulism, the cosmetic procedure is safe, they say, and no more painful than a visit to the hairdresser. (Note, I didn't say painless. A visit to the hairdresser can cause some suffering, actually. If you've ever had strands of your tresses pulled through a rubber cap with a crochet hook in the interest of something called "highlights," you know what I mean).

The original Botox does have one notable drawback, though. A little problem with the semi-permanent freezing of facial expression. Some Hollywood directors complain, in fact, that actors who have embraced Botox can no longer show the full range of human emotions required for their roles — but, hey, that's life, or something like it, in Tinsel Town. It's a small price to pay for vanity, $20-million-a-picture take-home pay and a box office gross that rivals some countries' GDP.

Still, that side effect is a neat metaphor for the rite of passage the average narcissistic boomer is now enduring.

We all seem a little desperate to capture time in a freeze-frame — to stop our faces in their tracks, as it were, to keep them looking as they did when they were callow and pure and unmarked by events.

It's not that we don't want experience. If ever there was a generation hungry for experience, it's the one born after the Second World War. We have always wanted to party. We have always wanted to test our limits. We even acknowledge that we might have to feel real pain from time to time. We just don't want it to show.

Other people age. But in the minds of many of my contemporaries, we are perpetually 19, wielding guitars and singing earnest protest songs in a convoy of VW microbuses meandering across the nation.

We demand to stay locked forever in the romantic turmoil of outraged youth, even as we see ourselves as seasoned and prudent. We believe it is our birthright. We want wisdom, all right. We just don't want the pesky nuisance of aging that usually comes with it.

The mirror doesn't know any of that, though. It tells us the truth, and the truth is tough on the ego.

Waxing philosophical is easier when the light is low and that heartless reflection is muted. I'd like to say with confidence that I'll never erase the lines my living has marked on my face. In an odd and contradictory way, I cherish them all.

But I'm a narcissistic boomer, too, and I know my own limitations. The day may come when I host a Botox party of my own. I don't mind going gentle into that good night. Not really. Like most of the people I know, though, I just want to look 20 when I finally do.

3 Sixty-five and punkin' it

"Fashion should be a form of escapism, and not a form of imprisonment"

— Designer Alexander McQueen (1969 – 2010)

She saunters through my neighbourhood with quiet confidence, wearing loud chartreuse shirts under louder magenta sweaters. A red in-your-face Indian scarf with inlaid mirror pieces swirls around her neck. Her leopard-print skirt swishes as she walks. Her unruly hair cascades in tight curls all the way down her back.

She must be 65 at least. The fashion police surely have a warrant out for her arrest. But if she ever gets apprehended, I will personally post her bail. She's my hero. She rejects The Uniform.

I am all too aware of the tyranny of The Uniform. The Uniform – the first of its kind – was a navy blue tunic with boxy pleats, cinched at the waist by two plastic buttons on a cloth belt. This shapeless monstrosity was worn atop a short-sleeved white cotton blouse that started out crisp but wilted by noon.

The whole enchanting get-up was finished with polyester navy knee socks and weighty blue Oxford lace-ups.

That was how we had to dress for school. The logic was that forcing us to wear identical outfits leveled the runway between the one per cent of students with industrialist parents and the remaining 99 per cent of us – the riff-raff.

It never really worked, of course. In the form of overloaded charm bracelets or jazzy earrings, bling found a way; it always does.

I had no bling. As a longstanding native of the riff and a card-carrying member of the raff, my own style at school wasn't exactly jaunty. In fact, I lived in a jaunt-free zone.

Still, I couldn't wait to learn how to express myself with a saucy scarf or an oh-so-European cloche hat. And I did. For 15 glorious unmarried, childless years, I had a disposable income and a developing eye.

More important, I was young. I had license to dress as wackily as I cared to.

I remember an era of something called elephant pants – extreme bell bottoms that swept the sidewalk clean of leaves. I had a yellow pair. I never thought twice about whether I could "carry them off." I felt free to hone my personal style, to forge my own fashion identity.

Then came the whole untidy, enriching upheaval of family life. Getting out of sweatpants constituted an occasion. When I did, I tended to opt for prim, almost matronly wear. After all, I was a matron.

During those years, dress had to do with conforming – setting an example by tamping down my wilder impulses. I didn't want to have to face the Harper Valley PTA.

By the time the kids were launched, I was into my 50s, single again and desperate to awaken my dormant sense of style.

But guess what? The pressure was on to return to standard attire. This time, the keepers of The Uniform consisted of a Star Chamber of fashion dictators. Their principal pronouncement to women of a certain age: Tone yourself down. And we've taken it to heart. Case in point. Don't let them fool you. Since most of my contemporaries seem to be dressing like elderly Sicilian widows, I think it's safe to say that black is still the new black.

The message is that if you're past your prime, you must dress like a crone and back away from the runway. Keep the skirt below the knee, the cleavage under wraps and the zebra jacket in the closet.

"A useful fashion tip [for those] over 60 is to keep it simple," reads one fashion blog. "Do away with large prints, multiple patterns and bright colours. Instead, opt for clothes in solid colours like black, blue, red, camel, khaki and white. These colours will not only make you appear slimmer, they will make you look elegant, too."

My view? Elegance is a euphemism. It really means "you're officially too old to carry off any other look."

Not me. I'm going to take a leaf out of my neighbour's underground version of *Vogue*.

I'm hiking up the skirt and dusting off my bright yellow sweater with the rhinestones. It's a little out there, yes. I'm a little out there, truth be told.

If I don't feel free to be a little out there now, when will I ever feel it?

4 Is it true blondes have more fun?

"There is only one cure for grey hair. It was invented by a Frenchman. It is called the guillotine."

— British humorist P.G. Wodehouse (1881-1975)

"The colour of truth is grey."

— Writer and Nobel laureate Andre Gide (1869-1951)

Sure thing, Mr. Gide. Try wearing "the colour of truth" to a job interview or on a blind date. Fifty shades of grey takes on a whole new twist for women in our age bracket. No matter how shimmering and silvery the locks, revealing them can somehow undermine confidence.

Yes, role models exist. Jamie Lee Curtis. Emmylou Harris. Dame Judi Dench. But for those of us with less stature, letting "truth" grow out of our scalps can be a scary proposition indeed.

Laura Hurd Clarke, PhD, an associate professor at the University of British Columbia, studies aging. She and a co-author conducted research in 2010 on the subject of grey hair. They polled 36 women over 70 to gauge their attitude to their manes. Most of them associated silver mops with "poor health, social disengagement and cultural invisibility."

"Women experience ageism based on looking older to a greater extent than men do," Clarke told a writer, exhibiting a great capacity for understatement. "Men can be the youthful Adonis or the distinguished older man, but there isn't an equivalent for women later in life. By and large, we don't have a cultural assumption that aging is beneficial to women's appearance."

Think of the language around grey hair. We talk about "exposing" our mature tresses as though we're planning to shimmy throughout the neighbourhood nude.

Yet according to some people, even walking down the street naked might not garner much attention, if the head attached to the body is slate-coloured. With grey hair, "you fade away into the background and no one sees you," said one 80-ish woman in Clarke's study. Better to hit the bottle, as it were. How about foxy mink or Arbutus red?

All of this is a relatively new phenomenon. My grandmother had grey hair fashioned into a classic knot at the back of her head. She wore it that way until the day she died. Her daughter, my mother, began dyeing her hair around the time she turned 50 and continued to do so until her death. That's because scientists developed less toxic dyes in the 1940s and beauty marketing really kicked into gear as Mom was reaching a certain age.

Colouring was safer, true, but not especially convincing. The flat matte look of painted tresses when my mother came home from the salon was a dead giveaway. It answered Clairol's famous question: She did.

She bought in to the hype all the same – and it seems like that's been the way of the world for women ever since. How rare it is to see proudly silver bobs or page boys among my contemporaries.

I began my addiction to the bottle in my 30s, when a strand here and there showed signs of losing its pigmentation. Colouring is refined nowadays and the palette has grown to include chartreuses and fuchsias for the truly intrepid.

I admit: I've experimented. Still, it's an odd sensation to have no idea how much grey covers my head. So I'm cautiously considering finally going natural. The cost of keeping up this sham is daunting. And who do I think I'm fooling?

I'm inspired by a friend who took the plunge. Her roots, carefully hidden in various fashionable hues for 30 years, are now "the colour of truth" and she swears she plans to hang in there.

Her friends are observing from afar, some in disbelief, others in awe. "You'll never make it," one said dismissively. The rest use terms usually associated with heroism. They cite her "courage" and her "pluck." They call her audacious, as though she'd climbed into a barrel destined for Niagara Falls. My feeling? Time has either won her over or worn her down.

Perhaps vanity softens around the edges as we age. Perhaps we're more inclined to give in to the inevitable. Maybe beauty hucksters have less impact. In any event, I sense a trend in the making – and I'm a boomer. I'm never wrong about these things.

PART 2: PASSING THE TIE-DYED MANTLE

5 The Plight of the Wal-Mart greeter

"Too many older workers, able and willing to enter new occupations, are wasting their time and talent on menial work or idleness. Too much of the contribution to our way of life which can only come from older men and women, is lost."

— John F. Kennedy (1917 – 1963)

When the Big Bust hit in 2008, several of my friends were sweating the envelope. The envelope held their latest investment statements and they dreaded opening it the way they had once dreaded the post-Christmas Visa bill.

Me? I was smug. No investments, therefore no fear. I was on an even keel – no poorer or richer than ever before.

The flip side, clearly, is that I hadn't prepared for my future. That meant I was likely to be earning my keep long after my friends' RRSPs had recovered and they were jetting off to extended vacations in Croatia.

That's a tad simplistic, of course. Not everyone bounced back after the crash. Figures indicate that when the derivative-driven dust had settled, Canada's private pension funds had lost more than 21 per cent of their value.

For those affected, visions of a rich and fruitful post-work period dissipated. They set their alarm clocks once more and began hunting for new jobs. Many experienced a rude awakening – emphasis on the word rude.

Some didn't make it to the interview process because they were seen as over-qualified.

Others were hired but exploited, demeaned and humiliated. They found themselves in part-time or temporary jobs. Or they were forced to accept far less than they were worth.

Half the older workers who returned to work after the big recession of 2008 saw their salaries drop by 25 per cent.

My earning power was hit hard for a long while, too, but I'm not complaining. I'm lucky that I can bring home the necessary bacon at my advanced age. With a keyboard and a few well-honed brain cells, I manage to earn a respectable living.

But for many Canadians in their 50s and 60s who still need to work, finding or keeping gainful employment is an ever-increasing challenge. Don't take my word for it. Those are the conclusions of a recently released report commissioned by the Canadian Association of Retired People (CARP).

If you're in our bulging cohort and you have a job, chances are you are clutching onto it. Statistics show that older Canadians are staying in the labour force longer than ever before.

Since 2000, there has been an 11 per cent uptick in the rate of citizens aged 65 to 70 who are earning salaries or are self-employed. That's a reversal of previous trends, especially for men.

Yet one-third of workers in that age bracket are "low wage," according to CARP. (The report doesn't specify what "low wage" means.)

What a waste. For a generation that perceives itself as laid back, it turns out we appear to be particularly industrious and diligent. That's the finding of a study released some time ago by EY, the financial services company formerly known as Ernst and Young.

EY polled more than 1,200 white-collar workers in the U.S. from different generations to try to determine what each group was thought to be good at – and where each was thought to be weak.

The report identified three cohorts – millennials aged 18 to 32, Generation X, aged 33 to 48, and baby boomers. As is usual in these surveys, what applies south of the border probably applies here, too.

Nearly 70 per cent of the respondents ranked baby boomers highest in terms of productivity and more than 73 per cent described us as "hardworking."

As well, more than half saw us as willing team players who are good at mentoring younger workers. Generation X just narrowly beat us out (80 per cent versus 76 per cent) in the "better managers" category.

However, boomers edged out Gen X as the best generation to "manage in challenging times" by a margin of four percentage points.

What's more, about two-thirds of those surveyed said our "executive presence" was terrific, whatever that means. (Perhaps we give good meetings.) At any rate, it's clear that in the workplace, we've still got it.

There *is* a downside. It seems we don't adapt to change easily. Just 12 per cent of respondents thought boomer managers were best at dealing with diversity – the poorest showing in the three groups.

Nor are we particularly flexible: less than one-quarter of those polled thought we excelled in that attribute.

Only 10 per cent of those questioned rated us high for adaptability. And a paltry 16 per cent cited "inclusive" leadership skills as a strong boomer trait. It seems the age group once known for breaking racial and sexual barriers has atrophied to some extent – at least, on the job, where conservative values appear to reign. Maybe it's inevitable. Maybe it's just sad.

Not surprisingly, the study also found millennials to be the most comfortable with new technology. Some 70 per cent of those polled said this group was the most likely to take full advantage of social media, compared with only six per cent of boomers and 24 per cent in the 33 to 48 age bracket.

But respondents also perceived this group to be slackers – not very good at generating revenue. Apparently, this newest generation in the workforce also doesn't have a reputation for building solid relationships on the job: just 13 per cent believe these whippersnappers play well with others.

And what about Gen Xers? The group following us seems to be taking charge with some authority. It is seen to be the best at managing, generating revenue, problem-solving and adapting to new techniques.

Its constituents excelled in the "collaboration" category, too, although they didn't fare well when it came to being regarded as earning their salaries. Their "executive presence" was found wanting, too. Guess they just don't have the gravitas that we possess – as of yet, anyway.

"While every individual is different," the authors of the study said, "the survey revealed perceived strengths and weaknesses of both the members and managers of each generation that can be instructive as companies work to effectively manage, engage and strengthen the generational mix."

Amen to that.

What's most encouraging about the findings is that – just as in society at large – a combination of wisdom and fresh ideas works together to help us move forward.

Young people can shake us out of our complacency and our hidebound biases. We, in turn, can teach them patience and the value of skill-building.

Yet too many employers appear to want to exploit us. That doesn't encourage us to give our jobs our best shot.

Even boomers who are well paid can find themselves in a nasty trap. I have a friend with a re- mortgaged house who is desperate to retire because her workplace has become foul and brutal. Recently hired younger people take these conditions as a matter of course, she says. So her bosses seem to suggest that if she can't keep up, she knows where the door is.

The bottom line, says CARP, is that "the right to work and remain engaged is under threat for many older Canadians."

Entrenched ageism pressures seniors out of the workforce "despite the benefits of their experience, skills and contributions to society."

The report goes on to say that "Many older workers feel ... their contributions are unvalued by employers."

Reality is harsh and Darwin rules. Survival of the fittest is the order of the day.

Those of us who do require an income to pay the daily freight have to coldly assess the marketplace and make all the right moves.

Some are resorting to plastic surgery. One Vancouver doctor reports that up to 60 per cent of his patients between the ages of 40 and 60 seek cosmetic treatments for work-related reasons. It gives the term job cuts a whole new meaning.

That's a little drastic, in my book. Yes – it's important to polish up the skills. But face it. We'll never be as nimble at social media as those who come after us.

Better to play to our strengths. And that would be our considerable experience. If only employers will let us.

6 If I don't pick up a pay cheque, who am I?

"Retirement at 65 is ridiculous. When I was sixty-five I still had pimples."

— George Burns (1896 – 1996)

But what about those who *can* afford to leave work but are reluctant to do so? Politicians don't much like to be booted out, but that doesn't stop us from booting them.

We like to see a changing of the guard. Whenever a new leader assumes residency in a stately government house, it gives us a shot in the proverbial arm. That's because we tend to imbue big institutional change with almost magical power.

New blood appeals. We expect it to revitalize us, to shake up the status quo, to get us going again, presumably in an onward and upward direction.

It's a different story, of course, when your own blood is getting on. Many of us who are charter members of that lumbering demographic known as the boomer generation are hitting a point in our lives when we have to come to terms with the idea of passing on the mantles we've been wearing.

Those of us moving through our 60s are at a tricky age – limber and vigorous, seasoned by years of honing our particular skills in our chosen fields.

Heck, we've been pretty well marinated in our work, absorbing the flavours that come from decades of victories little and large, blows to our egos, petty office politics and pats on our backs.

Yes, our faculties are playing tricks on us. We forget names, maybe, but never the nuances in tone and mood that can make all the difference in the Big Meeting.

We know our foibles and have dealt with them, or have maneuvered around them. We are in our work prime. Often, we make what we do look so easy, it can seem like we're coasting. Sometimes, truth be told, we do coast – but only because it took us years and years of building up enough momentum to allow us to, and still get the job done well.

We've paid our dues with pride and sweat. We know our craft in the very marrow of our being.

Then there are those coming up the ranks, nipping at our heels in the proper way of the world.

Boomer demographics being what they are, this batch of workers behind us isn't so young any more. Many have a kind of thirsty, honest ambition we recognize – we were there once ourselves. They are pulsing with new blood and brimming with shiny, bright notions.

But they worry they have nowhere to place their energy as long as we're sitting in the corner offices and making the big decisions.

Much as we may like the idea of nurturing protégés, they're tired of being mentored – of dealing with what they must feel is the know-it-all attitude of their so-called superiors.

So how do we find a balance? How do we make room for the new regime, while still making use of all our abilities? When is it best to cede the mantle and let others young and capable have a chance?

It's a tough call – hard to make because we're at the centre of the issue and our objectivity, of course, is in question.

Sometimes we don't even get to make the call ourselves – the decision is out of our hands.

But it's much harder when it falls to us individually to figure out when it's time to move on. Who really relishes the thought of being put out to pasture?

True, many people don't like their jobs and want to retire – just six per cent of Canadians work full-time after 65.

But for those of us who enjoy or need our work – or, indeed, need to work – the prospect of leaving a job doesn't sit well.

Apparently, there are enough of us and – as always – we have clout. Nine million Canadians born between 1946 and 1964 have strongly influenced public policy. That's why Canada has given the boot to mandatory retirement at age 65. Good for us. We're vital and energetic.

Still, forgive me, but it seems a little ironic that we coined the slogan "Never trust anyone over 30." Yet we appear to be having a hard time ceding the stage to the whippersnappers nipping at our heels.

Most of us have planned reasonably well for our so-called leisure years. All the same, far too many others – mea culpa – grew up in an era when the prevailing philosophy discouraged monetary considerations.

If you are at all like me, you may have had a lifelong struggle coming to terms with hard financial facts. I've never really bothered to crunch the necessary numbers. Thinking ahead wasn't my forte. But if I've failed to assume responsibility for my future, that isn't a valid reason for preventing my juniors from assuming responsibility for theirs.

So the real challenge becomes: How can we gracefully make room for them while still contributing? Here's one way of looking at the issue. Maybe we should be regarding the "pasture" in a whole new light. Sure, the expression has a negative connotation. A picture of cattle, placid and dull, blankly chewing on their cuds comes to mind. (Dairy cows, according to Wikipedia, are good for up to about 10 lactations before they go permanently off-duty, waiting to be culled. Not an inspiring image, that).

On the other hand, the "pasture" could give us a terrific vantage point to observe, absorb – and even to earn.

There's no doubt that we amassed a great deal of still-valuable expertise during our years in the workforce.

But we might have lost perspective when we made our careers our primary focus.

True wisdom comes from looking up and around. It is agenda-and ambition-free.

PART 3: REMEMBRANCE OF THINGS PAST

7 Surfing the genetic tide

"We're all ghosts. We all carry, inside us, people who came before us."

—American author Liam Callanan (b: 1968)

Petite and demure, she wears a mantle of lace around her shoulders over a full-length velvet dress. Her brow is high and wide, suggesting intelligence, and there is a hint of a Mona Lisa smile in her upturned lips. She is Rosa Gertrude Harris – the grandmother who died long before I was born – and I am her namesake, Victorian-era middle name included.

In the few sepia photographs I have of her, she is usually posed formally beside her somber-looking husband, Grandfather Felix, who is dressed in a conservative bespoke black suit. The jaunty handlebar moustache he sports seems his only vanity.

They had one child, my father Theodore, who died when I was just 10 years old. Theodore had no cousins, either. The family moved from Manchester, England, at the turn of the 20th century. Grandpa lived with us until he passed on when I was three. There is no extended family to share their secrets.

The truth is, I know so little about Rosa.

Apart from her photos, all that remains of her is a tarnished silver tray embossed with her name commemorating the good works she'd done as a volunteer in her short life. Perhaps that's why she haunts me in a gentle, provocative way, this woman I never met. She wants to know more about me, too.

I keep her pictures close on walls, shelves and mantles. I swear she eyes me every so often as if to determine whether or not her genes have had a soft landing.

When I catch her eye back, there is a familiar shock of recognition. Those commanding eyes, those lips – they belong to both of us. What else might we have shared, if I'd ever had the chance to find out?

Such notions never crossed my mind in my 20s, 30s or even 40s. Dead relatives – especially unfamiliar ones – weren't reaching out of gilded picture frames trying to get my attention. I was too busy making my own mark in this world – too busy giving her great-grandchildren and launching a career.

But she was patient. She knew the moment would come when a vague longing – a soft, urgent melancholy – would draw me back to her.

It seems we have to pass the halfway mark in our lives before thoughts of mortality kick in. I can now count the decades I have left on one hand – and I can imagine reaching out to my own kids from some photo taken long before. Just like me – big surprise – many boomers are entering a poignant phase, aiming to reconnect with their forebears.

Consider: Ancestry.com, the online, for-profit genealogy site, now has two-million members and branches in nine countries. (Here, it's known as ancestry.ca.) There are no figures available indicating how many of its users were born between 1945 and 1964, but I'm guessing we account for a good portion.

The service can eat hours – and we have the time. It's also costly – and we're the ones with enough money to delve into our pasts.

More important, we have this nagging urge to familiarize ourselves with relatives, distant and near, who just might be waiting to greet us in some fashion when we go.

Naturally, we romanticize when it comes to our ancestors. Of course, we want them all to be noble – in their actions if not in their blood. But that doesn't mean we should saw off the limbs on the family tree that hold the black sheep and the reprobates. They contribute colour and hearty genetic material to the mix.

In my own quest to learn more about Rosa, I hope I can unearth some flesh-and-blood tidbits that reveal her character, warts and all. If she was short-tempered or sharp-tongued, I can handle it. That's what would truly bring her alive. I must face the fact, though, that I may not discover enough about her to make her real.

But I can always fall back on those photos.

She's trying to tell me something. If I learn to listen, I'll eventually figure out what that is.

8 Where were you when?

"What is history but a fable agreed upon?"

— Napoleon Bonaparte (1769 – 1821)

Fuzzy analog footage, now more than a half-century old, took over the greying medium of network TV on the usual occasion last November. The date, of course, was the anniversary of the death of John Fitzgerald Kennedy.

His assassination forever shaped the collective adolescent psyche of the boomer nation.

What's more, the effect was permanent, maintains Carl Cavanagh Hodge, a professor of political science at the University of British Columbia. "Kennedy was cut down at the height of his popularity at a time when the baby-boom generation was arriving at political consciousness," he says. "It's not an exaggeration to say that many ... never wholly recovered from the shock."

I don't really know if I ever did. I was in Miss Wallace's Grade 7 class and I swear I can still smell the chalk in that room on that day.

When the school secretary came in and whispered something in Miss Wallace's ear, my strict disciplinarian of a teacher began sobbing – an oddly unnerving incident.

We were sent home early. As I walked up the steps, I could see the new Emerson console beaming eerie, flickering black-and-white images behind the living-room curtains. The set was on in the middle of the day – usually strictly forbidden and another incongruity. My mother was watching, transfixed. She held me when I arrived.

That was our cohort's earliest "where-were-you-when" moment – an event that was seared into our brains with a hot pitchfork. The end of the innocence – at least that's how we perceive it now.

In retrospect, the bullet that killed Kennedy seems to have been on a trajectory that led directly to upheaval in the 1960s. At the height of the TV broadcast era, we learned to identify more strongly with our age group than we did with Canadians at large.

By the time Robert Kennedy and Martin Luther King, Jr. were cut down, we were practically inured to hit men with a hatred of those with a microphone and a following. We got tougher and more cynical, less trusting and more wary.

You know you're getting older, though, when those "where-were-you-when" moments begin piling up, at least one per decade. After those assassinations, the War Measures Act in 1970 and Pierre Trudeau's defiant "Just watch me" statement were pivotal for me because I was living in Montreal and friends were getting caught up in police raids.

By the time of the Nixon resignation in 1974, I had my first newspaper job. I was assigned to pull a photo off the newswire. It showed the disgraced president boarding Air Force One for the last time, flashing peace signs and stressing the sleeves on his pathetically ill-fitting jacket.

Twelve years later, the space shuttle Challenger disintegrated in the sky 73 seconds after takeoff and 10 miles up. The tragedy was caught on tape and replayed again and again during prime time. I spent at least a week shielding my two-year-old from the footage, but an image of the long plume of smoke still resides somewhere in my brain. Even today, I can pull that picture out of my cerebral filing cabinet at will.

In the 1990s, the first Gulf War played out like a newfangled video game in real time on TV. I can still envision the night goggles American combatants wore that cast a ghoulish green glow on the dessert.

But for members of subsequent generations, most of these experiences are as remote to them as Pearl Harbor was to us. Certainly, what Gen-Xs and Gen-Ys know about JFK's death tends to revolve around kitschy conspiracy theories and a punk band with the provocative name Dead Kennedys.

As for millennials, their first touchstone image will always be the melting towers of 9/11 – and the horrific sight of desperate New Yorkers flying out their windows. For sheer terror, their primary political benchmark certainly one-ups ours.

Sadly, though, some new catastrophe will be etched onto the minds of their own children – and stories of that day in 2001 will leave no permanent mark on the souls of the new generation.

The reality is this: Life right now is as sharp as the latest flat-screen monitor. History is always veiled in snow and static.

9 It's my nostalgia – and I'm sticking to it

"The world is full of people whose notion of a satisfactory future is, in fact, a return to the idealized past."

— Canadian author Robertson Davies (1913 – 1995)

Look behind you 40 years and what do you see? In my case, the foggy ruins of time reveal a cheeky young girl wearing huge purple bell bottoms, a flowing paisley tunic – and copping lots of attitude. She is so free of the torpedo bras and constricting girdles that defined her mother's life that she takes all freedom for granted. How accurate? Who knows? But it's my nostalgia – and I'm sticking to it.

In a recent *New Yorker* magazine, writer Adam Gopnik made a compelling argument. He called it the Golden 40-year Rule – and he posited that "the prime site of nostalgia is always whatever happened, or is thought to have happened, in the decade between 40 and 50 years past."

He offered, as an example, the *Mad Men* series. The juggernaut of a TV hit that concluded in 2015 was stylized and polished. Set in the remarkable transition years of the early-to-mid 1960s, the original seasons might as well have been shot in black and white. Fedoras, Scotch and illicit office affairs are the principal props.

By Season Five we're in the mid-sixties and the set is awash in candy colours and polka dots. The mood is lighter, vibrant and almost wacky. Sounds about right to me.

Gopnik suggests there's a reason for his golden rule. Those in their 40s and 50s, he says, are in their prime creative period. They drive popular culture.

Presumably, as observant, young ankle-biters, their first memories and sensations made indelible impressions that are now being played out on screen.

He adds that "the manners and meanings" of our own era will only truly be revealed in the 2050s. It will take until then, he says, before "we know our own essence."

In my Kindle, ours is an era of transition, too.

So here's my shot at helping the toddlers of today define five elements of that "essence" when it's their turn to look back:

• **The transition from mass to agility.** Those middle-aged in the mid-21st century will regard physical books and records as quaint artifacts in much the way we now think of milkmen on horse-drawn carts. Unencumbered and lithe, our grandchildren will marvel at the burden we carried whenever we moved, weighed down in thought and in action.

• **The transition from cash to digits.** Four or five decades down the road, I'm guessing people will collect paper money the way our dads and brothers once collected stamps. Commercial transactions will be conducted in a biometric wink of the eye at warp speed. Seconds lost at old-fashioned cash registers would be inconceivable in a just-in-time economy.

• **The transition from gender to androgyny.** *Vive la similarité.* Future generations will puzzle and guffaw over the way we made distinctions between men and women. Gender chameleons are already becoming more common among the young. Check out college campuses now and watch how many students in their 20s play with sex roles. Our descendants won't blend to the point of bland, though. Flamboyant dress and make-up will rule.

• **The transition from prosthetics to bionics.** Glasses? Hearing aids? Wooden limbs? By mid-century, these items will be cluttering up antique stores and yard sales. Down the road, synthetic, nerve-controlled knee bones will seamlessly connect to natural thigh bones. Sight and other senses will not just be corrected – they'll be enhanced for those who can afford procedures. And that suggests one final trend that will probably reach maturity in half a century:

• **The transition from middle class back to a sharply stratified society.** Looking back at our day, pop culture enthusiasts will see winners and losers and those who just muddled through.

My suspicion is that muddling won't be much of an option for our progeny's progeny. They will either be of the manor born or they will be scrambling for meager leftovers.

It's hard to see ourselves in context along the timeline of history.

And everyone knows prediction is a mug's game. Future generations will no doubt put us in our proper place.

But I'm a mom. I can't resist helping them with their homework.

10 Heirlooming large

"I still feel pangs of remorse over an insidious habit I've had since I was a teenager. About three times a week, I attend estate auctions and make insulting, low-ball bids for prized heirlooms until I'm asked to leave."

— American comedian Dennis Miller (b: 1953)

Truly wicked, that Dennis Miller. How dare he make a mockery of a family's heritage? So what if that heritage manifests as a set of tacky Royal Doulton ballerina figurines or as a clunky pine sideboard from the Old Country? We have an instinct and a craving to pass on objects that are meaningful to us, infused as these items are with intangible history.

And yet. Try dragging a ton-and-a-half of heirlooms – that's 1,361 kilograms – all across the country. That's what I did, when I moved to British Columbia from the east.

They were my father's books – and they lined the library in my childhood home where I whiled away many hours on his lap. Together, we would thumb through atlases of the Earth and schemata of the night sky. He died when I was 10. These tomes had absorbed his tobacco smoke and his aftershave and were a palpable reminder of the fundamental curiosity he awakened in me – as a kid and forever. The books were, always, tacitly, mine after he was gone.

Over the years, sitting in basement storage boxes, many became musty and moldy. And even those that were kept out of the damp often suffered cracked bindings, their pages decaying into fragile, powdery crepe.

Every time I moved, I'd assess them again. Many of the volumes were hefty, obsolete encyclopedias or middlebrow novels of the forties and fifties that hadn't aged well. What's more, the scent of my father was becoming ever more remote. Gradually, I've begun dispensing with them. I cart them off to secondhand sellers who often dismiss them, gently, as worthless. So I put some in library drop boxes in hopes they will find a home. I suffer pangs every time.

Several still remain with me – mementos and amulets. They were hard to give up, at first. Now, I'm not sorry I did.

On a shelf in my kitchen are four or five elegant fine bone china cups and saucers – one of my mother's many heirloom presents to me. What possessed her to keep them is unclear. By the time they were hers to give, they meant little to her, too. They were from my father's long-gone side of the family and their provenance was unknown. The numbered inscription on their underside had worn away.

They might have been part of my grandmother's trousseau – but who could tell? When I was a kid, they were already gathering dust in a cabinet, deemed far too fussy for a modern mid-century household.

Still, although I had no qualms selling the Moorcroft vase and the silver tea set, I carry these cups with me everywhere. I don't know why I feel a powerful link to them.

Keepsakes can be a burden and a yoke, imbued with time, memory, guilt and sorrow. Or they can trigger a visceral connection that we find impossible to forfeit, even as their meaning dulls and fades.

"It is difficult to put into words when you find war medals of courage and valour left on the floor for disposal, or antique photos of people in the family that have been left in a pile for us to discard," writes Texas estate sales expert Julie Hall in her blog. "But we understand that every person has a story and we are not privy to their upbringing or lives, and therefore do not understand why they made the decisions they did."

I used to wonder which items – if any – I would pass on to my own children. And which would they find impossible to discard? Doubtful the microwave oven or the circa 1970s blender. Boomers grew up in an era of disposability, when newer and better goods were always a virtue. As that attitude accelerates with each generation, I had to wonder whether heirlooms, as a notion will survive.

Then my son came to visit. Talk turned to an old filing cabinet of mine, full of typewritten notes and drafts of stories I'd written over the years. He was horrified to learn that I had tossed this appendage, contents and all, into the local dump. His reaction surprised and touched me. Perhaps this was the heirloom he would have kept once I was gone.

I'd short-changed him and felt instantly sorry for what I'd done. Apparently, sentimentality is not quite the antique I presumed it to be.

11 Regrets, I have a few . . .

"Make the most of your regrets; never smother your sorrow, but tend and cherish it till it comes to have a separate and integral interest. To regret deeply is to live afresh."

— Henry David Thoreau (1817 – 1862)

"Ask an older person you respect to tell you his or her greatest regret."

— American author H. Jackson Brown, Jr. (b: 1940)

Mr. Thoreau's approach to regret is unusual.

If you don't believe me, consider this a dare. Do a search for quotations about regret on Google, as I did.

Discount this kind of regret: not saying 'I love you' enough, missing a kid's school performance, not buying the right car.

Instead, look for observations about deep regret – the kind caused by someone's heedless role in events that changed people's lives for the worse.

My own finding was this: we're not big on regret.

A quick look at 19 pages of pithy and startling statements made by figures ranging from Jimi Hendrix to Adolf Eichmann produced only a handful that acknowledged regret for past actions.

Eichmann's remark wasn't among them. "To sum it all up," said one of the major architects of the Holocaust, "I must say I regret nothing."

You'd expect such banal evil from a psychopath, granted. But as for the others, I found it odd that regret was something so many actively and avidly denied.

Typically, you find declarations such as this one from the writer Katherine Mansfield: *Make it a rule of life never to regret and never to look back. Regret is an appalling waste of energy. You can't build on it. It's only good for wallowing in.*

What gives with regret? In other respects, this is an era of emotional ascendency, a time when every dime store self-help guru urges us to carve our hearts out of our chests and apply same, while still pumping, to our sleeves.

"Instead of stuffing feelings of frustration down, address them and exaggerate them," advises a therapist on one website.

"Honour your anger," declares another. "Let it loose within the safety of your room."

But ask most people to own up to a major misstep in their past and they're likely to get stubborn and defensive. They come at you with their dukes up, angling for a fight if you challenge them.

Non, said Edith Piaf defiantly, *Je regrette rien.*

We're a litigious society. If a company or a government apologizes for past actions, lawsuits erupt like acne on a teenybopper's face – so perhaps there's been a trickle-down effect when it comes to admitting our personal wrongs.

Or maybe the reason we don't embrace regret is because it's a pentimento of an emotion, layered and subtle, not easy to pin down and express.

At any rate, it should come as no surprise, I suppose, that human nature seeks to ditch regret.

We can't change the past. What's the point, as Ms. Mansfield asserts, of wallowing in it?

That's a cop-out, in my view. The hard truth? Who really wants to concede to a long-ago fall from grace?

One study on the subject found that "people are remarkably good at avoiding self-blame, hence they may be better at avoiding regret than they realize."

And what makes this avoidance particularly relevant to our age group is how skilled we are at it.

According to psychologists Neal J. Roese and Amy Summerville, who wrote a paper called *What We Regret Most ... and Why*, our cohort has learned very well how to kick regret to the curb.

They cite one study that showed that the older we get the more averse we are to dealing with personal actions from our pasts. "As [people's] own opportunities fade with advancing years," they write, "so too do the most painful and self-recriminating regrets, to be replaced instead by 'neutered' regrets that emphasize the actions of other people." In other words, we're finding fault with others, rather than looking inward.

Yet the authors also note "regret pushes people toward revised decision-making and corrective action that often bring improvement in life circumstances."

That's why I beg to differ with Ms. Mansfield and side with Mr. Thoreau. I cherish my regrets.

I won't let mine atrophy with age. I don't sweat the small ones – the thoughtless word here and there or the occasional drink too many.

But frankly, I embrace the big ones, triggered by events that left me hunting for my moral compass in the dark.

I own those regrets. I revisit them with some regularity.

And yes, I wallow in them when the mood strikes. Why? They remind me of a time I put my principles to the test and failed the exam. Regrets have allowed me a do-over.

Today they keep me honest and upright.

Part 4: HOPE I DIE BEFORE I GET OLD

12 A Walk on the Wild side

"Swim upstream. Go the other way. Ignore the conventional wisdom."

— American businessman Sam Walton (1918 – 1992)

Call it a severe case of acute February that carries on for 12 months. Its primary symptom is stasis. Just as winter wears us down physically, the brain in the final season of our years tends to get salty and crusty, prone to falling back on conventional wisdom. Arthritis of the mind is dangerous. To help you fight off the complacency bug, your Aunt Rosa now offers the following naturopathic treatments:

• Release your annoying inner contrarian. At a recent dinner party, conversation turned to a political talk show that had everyone riled up. The program had pitted a gang of the usual suspects against an opposing gang of same. Natch, the issue at hand was deemed to be of profound social importance. As we nibbled on organic greens that evening, all of us weighed in. One diner was arch, another strident, a third calm and reasoned. Oh, we were pithy. Oh, we were sharp. Oh, we were predictable.

How so? Every one of us – except for that silent guy in the corner – took the requisite left-coast umbrage at the right-wing views expressed by the wrong tribe of panelist.

Lacking the courage to challenge, I found myself longing for some Christopher Hitchens–style bad boy to come barreling in, laying intellectual waste to our casual orthodoxy. Debate and the banter that it generates get the juices flowing. Consensus is not sexy. Next time I'm in that situation, I swear I'm going to lead with my chin. Honest.

• Get blotto. You have just learned that your mother-in-law and your slacker 30-year-old daughter are vying for the very rental suite that until now has brought you in a cool grand a month. Those days of extra cash are likely over and you will now be living in a whinery.

Listen to Auntie Rosa: Try this at home (and nowhere else). Pick an indulgence – any indulgence. Then, overindulge, with abandon. Wolf down three cream puffs. Chug-a-lug that fourth glass of scotch. For one crazy evening, throw caution to the wild winter wind and go a little nuts. Make a concerted effort to undo decades of constraint, moderation and hyper-responsibility. Do so alone. Do so with a like-minded soul. But in one short burst, do so. Will you suffer tomorrow? You bet. A little suffering is good for the soul. We ache, therefore we are.

• Plan a little mischief. Construct an elaborate practical joke – one involving GPS and a horse, perhaps – that takes weeks to unfold.

Or, invent a conspiracy theory. Make it just plausible enough. Here's an example to get you thinking. Did you know Wall Street was behind the Occupy movement because it wanted to demonstrate the sheer ineptitude of the

99 per cent? In fact, corporate bigwigs sent moles into city parks to further disorganize the motley band of ragtag protesters. And those famous Occupy hand signals? They're code that tells traders in the know when to buy and sell. You get the general idea.

Now, paste your theory on your Facebook page. Tell your 340 friends that your source for this info was your broker.

Advise them to spread the word. Giggle when a stranger repeats it back to you as fact three weeks hence.

• Cultivate mystery. Disappear without explanation for a half day after you've faithfully promised to meet an unsuspecting friend. Don't call or get together until she contacts you. When you finally do meet, make an effort to look flushed, disheveled – and hope she notices. If she does ask, blush and mumble something implausible. Begin throwing foreign words into your conversation. French is good, but Japanese is even better. Order exotic cocktails that call for absinthe and Ouzo.

If you're a woman, start wearing a cloche with a veil, but only indoors. (If you're a man, however, don't even bother giving this advice a shot. You are inherently incapable of mystery. Women can read you like a downloaded dime-store novel.) The message here: If you want to reduce the look of fine lines and wrinkles by 63 per cent, slather on the expensive face cream if it makes you feel better.

But the real secret elixir of youth, in my mind, is avoiding smug sameness. Shake things up. Bring a little outrage to the party.

Everyone knows walking is great exercise. Why not take a short one on the wild side? It's just across the street.

13 Forever Young

"May God bless and keep you always,

May your wishes all come true,

May you always do for others

And let others do for you,

May you build a ladder to the stars

And climb on every rung,

May you stay forever young"

— Bob Dylan (b: 1941)

Okay. Can you stand yet another take from yet another codger noting the fact that Dylan will soon turn 75?

Can you deal with another duffer who has come to some kind of naïve and startled recognition that time – are you ready for it – passes?

Can you cope with another aging boomer waxing nostalgic about the Sixties?

You can't, you say? Live with it. Age has all too few rewards. The freedom to rant is one of them.

You kids out there think you know what irony is? Dudes. Get real. Dylan practically invented the notion all by himself. But he was at his best when he dropped the irony in favour of unadulterated sentiment.

In his heyday, Dylan may have been the master of cool, but he was still able to get under your skin so much, he made you want to shed it just to see what it was doing underneath.

So maybe you bled a little in the process. You heal quickly when you're still in your 20s.

You wear the scars of love and loss with pride as you come of age. They're a mark of fearlessness, born of the confidence that you're immortal.

Forever young. Hah. At that age, you can't imagine the alternative.

Still, Dylan wrote the song when he was 34, no longer the stripling middle-class snot-nosed kid from Hibbing, Minnesota who'd elbowed his way to the top of the pop heap by glibly manufacturing a highly marketable hobo persona.

Dylan was on the cusp of middle age himself, with a marriage on the wane, a bevy of squawking kids and a career in some kind of perpetual flux.

He wrote it at the very moment his wounds were first taking all the time they needed to fester. It was a particularly poignant song under the circumstances.

"May you grow up to be righteous,

May you grow up to be true,

May you always know the truth

And see the lights surrounding you,

May you always be courageous,

Stand upright and be strong

May you stay forever young"

Man, could Dylan wield a lyric back then, in his prime. His words could drip with sarcasm. His love songs could open a vein. And when you least expected it of him, he would drop all his posturing, strip away every last shred of artifice and pierce your heart with an anthem so universal that it still resonates like no one's business 39 years from the get-go.

In fact, *Forever Young* is all the more bittersweet when you have to listen to it with a hearing aid.

We'd all like to feel that we've grown up to be righteous and truthful, courageous and filled with light.

Put any of us to the test, though, and you'll find that we tend to dwell on our failures of will and spirit, that we're all too familiar with the dark side of our souls, that we're still filled with longings that we may never have the time or the guts to face head on.

Forever young. You may appreciate the sentiment deeply. You'd like to believe that you can still see the world with wide and infant eyes.

But by now, most of us boomers wear progressive lenses in our glasses – and that tends to affect the purity of our vision.

"May your hands always be busy,

May your feet always be swift,

May you have a strong foundation

When the winds of changes shift

May your heart always be joyful

May your song always be sung

May you stay forever young."

It's hard to be both innocent and experienced at once, as Dylan's song seems to demand of us.

It's hard to remember the last time we felt anything for the first time.

It's hard to find ourselves shuffling when we feel like dancing in the wind.

It's hard to maintain hope and dreams and optimism in the face of approaching twilight.

But hang on a moment. Our hands are still busy and our feet, sheathed in the latest Nike Flyknits, are swifter than ever.

We've built our foundations on as solid ground as you're going to find these days.

And we still get our fair share of deeply joyful moments, to boot. So we're still singing Dylan's song.

Deal with it, children – deal with it.

14 Alice down the rabbit hole

"If you chase two rabbits, both will escape."

—Anonymous

"Give whatever you are doing and whoever you are with the gift of your attention."

—Jim Rohn, American entrepreneur (1930 - 2009)

Please bear with me – and I promise you, that won't be easy in the current environment.

I sat down to write this piece. I got up after 20 seconds to feed the dog. I sat down to write this piece. I got up after a minute and a half to throw a load of wash into the dryer. I sat down to write this piece. I remained sitting, but my e-mail buzzer went off and broke my focus. I switched screens to reply.

Since I was already on the Net, I punched "concentration" into Google to see what minds greater than mine had to say about the subject. That led to a tangential goose chase through the back 40 of cyberspace – through newly tilled earth strewn with absorbing trivia, instant wisdom and bad jokes. I looked at the clock. I'd eaten up two vital hours.

The prevailing word for this kind of hyperactivity is "multi-tasking" – a benevolent-sounding term that makes a flibbertigibbet feel more like a one-man orchestra, skillfully maneuvering a cymbal, a guitar and a mouth organ simultaneously.

But really, the noise it caused was cacophony. If there was a consistent, melodic tune – a genuine, fully realized theme to my thinking – it was hard to locate amidst all the mental debris. Raise your hand if you've been there.

The worry here is that the modern world has made dilettantes of us all; we've sacrificed pure deliberation on a digital altar composed of appropriately named bits and bytes. Information flows through our fingertips with the power of a tsunami.

Look for one relevant reference in a search engine and find 150 more, each demanding we come to rest on it, however fleetingly. And the effect has permeated the rest of our endeavours. Distraction has become a way of life.

It is the era of attention deficit disorder, a fashionable condition said to affect four per cent of the population and one that has given rise to a whole new class of drugs. We're not just talking kids, here. We're talking CEOs and politicians and health workers and pundits. But I submit that the situation is epidemic – more the order of the day than the exception.

Consider what doctors have defined as some of the symptoms: lack of focus, daydreaming, easily bored, difficulty completing tasks and processing information.

Any of that ring a bell?

Before we hit the medicine cabinet for the Ritalin, though, perhaps we should take a hard look at the devices and their content that got us here in the first place.

Take away my computer and hear me howl. Still, I recognize the impact it has had on my ability to, for example, read a story through from beginning to end, to give the gift of my full attention to a writer who is asking for it. Pity the poor souls who try to mount an argument and see it through. They've lost us, more often than not, after the first blue phrase appears in their work.

All those hyperlinks (the operative part of that word is "hyper") beckon and we might never make it back to the original material. Their theses become road kill on the information highway.

In his seminal book, *The Gutenberg Elegies*, Sven Birkerts wrote of electronic media: "impression and image take precedence over logic and concept, and detail and linear sequentiality are sacrificed." And he wrote that in 1994, long before the Internet took over our consciousness.

This affects our emotional world, too.

Looking for new love? There's a smorgasbord of souls out there on all the dating sites. How do we choose when there are so many to choose from?

It's a matter of time, I suggest, before Big Pharma identifies another syndrome. Call it RADD – Relationship Attention Deficit Disorder. Any day, there'll be a pill for that.

Reining in our brains and our hearts is no easy task. But if we're ever to make order out of chaos – to recognize the value of context – reclaiming our powers of concentration may well be Job One... Now, where was I?

15 The Graduate

"When first I saw a sheepskin,

In Johnson's hands I spied it,

I'd give my hat and boots, I would,

Just to have been beside it,

Oh! When examinations past,

We've skinned and fizzled through

With lectures done and prizes won,

We'll have our sheepskin too."

— University drinking song, circa 1882

They don't give out much sheepskin on campuses at the moment – animal rights and all.

In this era's version, the product of choice is embossed parchment, stamped with a shiny red official seal and neatly signed by the chancellor and the president.

OK, you wise guys out there. If you want to get crassly technical, today's university degree is issued on a measly 8-by-11-inch piece of pulp and paper. It isn't even rolled up. Or in regal Latin. But it does come in a pretty coloured envelope. And it is suitable for framing.

At any rate, the words on the paper can still raise a goose bump or two. I know. I didn't give my hat and boots for one of those babies. But I did give a few good years of my prime.

Maybe that's why, despite my urge to stomp on pomp on principle, I'm still a sucker for a good graduation ceremony. As rituals go, there aren't too many to beat this annual university event for history and tradition.

Those grim-reaper-style outfits parading to the podium in 2015, for example, were also the grads' garb of choice in the 14th century. Medieval scholars were the first to wear the get-ups – most likely to stay warm in the unheated stone buildings where they studied. The look clearly caught on. Now they even use them in *Scream* movies.

I'm a particular sucker for this event at Carleton University, my alma mater. (As rarely as I use that term, it always feels good when I do.)

It was raining and 30-plus when I graduated at a considerably advanced age clutching a Master's degree in journalism. Despite the heat, I still got to wear the familiar black gown, complete with a hood lined in silver and striped in ebony and red to signify my accomplishment.

My family, who had lost me for several years to miserable take-home exams, caffeinated all-nighters and an interminable thesis on an arcane subject – copyright – was sweating at my side. Their collective sigh was audible in the crowded stadium. They had suffered. They had survived. So had I. Barely.

The euphemism for students like me, I'd learned when I registered, was "mature." It meant of course, "old" not "wise." It also meant rusty, cranky, conservative – not to mention short a few zillion brain cells compared to the snot-nosed kids in the cohort.

And boy, do you feel all of the above when you have to contend with passages such as this: "Weber defines modernity in terms of the rationality of means, as opposed to the rational goal of values. In more concrete terms, he contrasts the ethic of responsibility, which characterizes modern man, with the ethic of conviction which, like charismatic authority, can intervene in a rationalized world only in exceptional circumstances." That's from a little page-turner called *Critique of Modernity*, by Alain Touraine. Today, I say to you: huh?

But back then I thought I knew what it meant. For a while, I probably did.

Not that I was ever really into what they call the academic idiom.

I'm a classic boomer. Which is to say that in the years I was supposed to be getting my undergraduate degree, I was banging my head to the sound of Hendrix's *Purple Haze* and wailing along with Joplin as she bleated Gershwin's *Summertime*.

Life was a simple joy at 19, a joy that didn't include school. Hey, it was 1969. So I never did get to wear that gown in my 20s. Not that I'd have even considered it back then. I would have thought the ceremony just too bourgeois for words.

Still, by the time I hit late midlife and after decades as a journalist, I felt the urge to finally get wise – to take a break from practice long enough to cop a little theory.

Despite the big gap in my resume where "education" should have been, Carleton took me into the fold, accepting my years in the field in lieu of an undergraduate degree.

Now, looking back, I can tell you I loved every last minute of my time there, Touraine and all, even when my first mark – 14 out of 20 – made me cry.

I reveled in the luxury to think.

I got a huge kick out of the brains and the irreverence of the whippersnappers – and made friends for life with the students my age.

My teachers were superior.

My mind was sharpened.

My appreciation for tradition was honed.

Parchment-shmarchment. I have my sheepskin too.

16 Kindling the reading flame

"Properly, we should read for power ... The book should be a ball of light in one's hand."

— American poet Ezra Pound (1885-1972)

"Well, something's lost and something's gained in living every day."

— Singer-songwriter Joni Mitchell (b. 1943)

The book as a ball of light in the hand. Only a poet could come up with the notion.

No wonder Ezra Pound had a rep for being a master of imagery – for applying "vivid or figurative language to represent objects, actions, or ideas."

That's the dictionary definition. In my own sense of the term, imagery means language that exhorts us to visualize using only our inner eye.

Avid readers know that's more fun than it sounds.

Think about your favourite fictional characters in novels. I bet you can describe details of their "lives" down to their ex-spouse's middle names and their preferred ice cream flavours.

Creating a mental picture out of symbols on a page is a leisurely, highly personal exercise. The process fires the imagination.

And if the words are commanding, a full-scale blaze takes hold. We use that fuel to inspire us – to give us the power Pound speaks of.

Some of us, of course, have always read strictly for pragmatic reasons – to absorb abstract concepts or merely for instruction and explanation.

Still, the act involves some kind of magic. We lift ideas off paper and put them through the factory in our brains until out they come through our mouths or on our computer screens with value added.

But here's the thing. Ours may be the last generation to find solace, joy or plain, unvarnished facts in this way.

Words, in all their grace and glory, are losing their impact.

A depressing statistic that gives heft to this argument suggests that by 2031, more than 15-million Canadian adults will have low literacy levels. That means they will only be able to handle simple, clear material involving uncomplicated tasks. (The study was conducted by the Canadian Council on Learning. The council itself was defunded in 2011 by the federal government. Perhaps bureaucrats in Ottawa had difficulty understanding the grant proposal.)

Should we freak out, to use '60s vernacular? It depends on whom you ask.

Some social theorists are despairing. One is an American essayist, Sven Birkerts. "Literature and old-style contemplative reading seem enfeebled," he writes, "almost as if they need to be argued for, helped along by the elbow."

But others – several of whom are neuroscientists – suggest we're merely adapting to a new order, a world far more visually oriented than the one we grew up in.

This line of discussion says our brains are being rewired to prefer immediate data from graphics over cryptograms that have to be decoded. The former cuts out a step, don't you know.

Evidence of this abounds. Nowadays, sentences, paragraphs, stories and the information we expect them to convey are being supplanted by charts, illustrations and Internet mini-movies.

Every factoid we inhale seems to come wrapped in elaborate, dynamic graphics – even manuals for new gadgets.

Just try downloading instructions for your new cellphone in booklet form. It's more than likely you'll first run into some inarticulate doofus who's produced an equally inarticulate YouTube video on the subject. Yeesh!

How to explain this trend? Put it down to our kids who went to school when teaching methods were revolutionized.

The pedagogical flavour of the era was "learning styles."

The theory was that certain children were better equipped to absorb information through visual cues than through written material.

The movement began 30 years ago and has since been largely debunked, but not before a good portion of our offspring ditched books in favour of pictures.

On top of that, callow cynics will tell you, words have been used to obfuscate and confuse a largely gullible society.

Throw in the filmic thrill of video games and it's not surprising many young adults have little patience with sheets of pure type.

Me? Almost in spite of myself, I've become enthused by the way cool diagrams and colourful infographics can tell a story.

But I'm keeping my inner eye wide open.

The silent exchange I have with great writers is still the only thing that can truly fire my imagination.

17 Action!

"Time is a moving target."

– Rosa Harris (b: 1950)

Money will let you down.

There's rarely enough of it. And even when we think we're flush, the coin of the realm has a way of evaporating steadily. Steam in a pot of soup.

Stocks shed their value like a cocker spaniel sheds on your carpet. The equity you've worked so hard to build in your home is subject to the vagaries of the real estate market. Lose your job and your nest egg is forced to hatch before it's had a chance to fully incubate.

Enough of the mixed metaphors. Bottom line, you can't count on money.

Ah, but time is constant. Sure, it expands and contracts according to circumstance and mood – remember how summer stretched endlessly the moment that school let out in June?

But know this. We are all allotted a tiny portion of minutes and hours. The clock is always ticking.

True, we have more of it on our hands these days. The kids are launched. We're winding down on the career front. Our schedules are not as crowded as they once were. Don't be deceived all the same. Time is about as finite as it gets.

Another aspect of life that won't let you down is community – unless you let it down. So here's a thought. Why not use any new-found time to enhance yours?

In recent years, the Caledon Institute of Social Policy, a private non-profit charitable foundation, has been exploring how to foster municipal engagement.

One of its findings: People's energy and commitment to community building are best unleashed when they drive the process and are allowed to organize their efforts with others.

In other words, getting involved in your community is empowering. It pays to earn your place in your neighbourhood.

Here are some first-step suggestions for making that engagement happen:

– Take the bus. Choose a route near you and ride it from one end to the other, making stops along the way. Learn something about the history of the enterprises and residences you pass. Find out who lived in these areas 50 or 100 years ago, what businesses have come and gone.

Talk to the driver. If you're constantly hermetically sealed in your car, you'll never get a feel for the place where you live.

– Attend a city council meeting or two. Sessions can be improv theatre at its best. True, you might nod off during discussions of picayune bylaw details. But take note of how your representatives interact. Who's a consensus builder? Who's grandstanding? What important issues are being swept under the rug? You'll feel better armed to vote come the next municipal election.

– Volunteer. Becoming a board member with a literacy group or a homeless shelter is one way to go, certainly. But more immediate, one-on-one action can be satisfying, too. Offer your skills as a tutor, a lawyer, a cook. Do the grocery shopping for an elderly woman. Find one person in your community who needs your help.

– Learn the names of 10 people in your neighbourhood. Start talking across the fence. Chat with the woman who runs the used bookstore. Engage the friendly busker in conversation. Build relationships.

The more people you know on your block, the more cohesive your block becomes. And the next time there's a local issue – say, a dangerous crosswalk that needs addressing – the easier it will be to mobilize people.

– Support your local media. Taking out a subscription for your struggling local daily is one way to do it, of course. But pick up your community weekly newspaper, too, and keep your eyes peeled for publications produced by the homeless population: many municipalities have one.

Watch the city's television stations. Check out the work of local bloggers.

Get the buzz on the street. If you want to become part of the conversation, it helps to know what's being said.

You've heard of the 100-mile diet. Think of all this as 100-mile activism.

18 Reviving the dream

"Youth would be an ideal state if it came a little later in life."

— Herbert Henry Asquith, British Prime Minister (1852 - 1928)

It's a crime and a joy what children do to you. They sap you in your prime. They demand that you give up the harebrained dream — admit it — that you secretly harboured in your early-adult heart.

Surely, you remember the dream. You were going to drop everything and move to New York. You were going to write a breakthrough book. You were going to paint, or discover, or sing, or invent, or undermine the system, or run for parliament. You were going to do all of the above, set the world on its ear and make it beg for more.

Suddenly, there the children were, pink and squalling and cooing. There were ear infections that kept you up all night. There was homework that needed supervising. There was life insurance to buy, pushing you onto the straight and narrow, chained to a job that paid the freight.

You quickly discovered that you didn't discipline kids. Kids disciplined you. All the unfocused energy that had gone into campus politics and protests was now laser-beamed on the task of making life secure for the little ones. Everyone but the most ambitious or driven gave in to the sweet, messy inevitable, too tired and preoccupied to contemplate the remarkably ordinary turn life had taken.

In the wake of diapers and day care, perhaps you abandoned the dream without even noticing.

Maybe it retreated to a corner of your consciousness, surfacing from time to time like a starved phantom in the middle of the night. Maybe it atrophied.

Well, take a good look around. The kids are launched. The day job is winding down.

And our huge, lumbering demographic – those of us born between 1945 and 1960 – is wondering what to do next.

And as we wonder, the dream begins to gnaw at the rusting shackles of responsibility that kept it down all those years.

We have an option here. We can put the dream out of its misery or we can let it loose. We can take a long rest until the end of our days, or we can act. We can bask in the bounty we've been graced with, or we can do. We can dismiss as the callow misadventure of youth the idealism that helped end a war in Southeast Asia, or we can own it.

Listen to Ron Kovic, the paralyzed Vietnam veteran who became and remains a fist-shaking anti-war activist. His autobiography, "Born on the Fourth of July," was turned into a hit film.

"We have every reason to be proud," he said of the boomer cohort. "We were brash and bold and beautiful."

He isn't disheartened by the way our passions were put on hold as we went about keeping the wheels of society greased. In fact, he feels that we're on the verge of rediscovering our revolutionary fervour – and that we'll give the term "the sixties" a whole new meaning. "Often when people get older, they say to the younger generation, 'Well, it's your turn now,'" he said. "I feel very differently. Rather than just passing the torch, and saying we did our best, this generation – which dreamed such big, impossible dreams – refuses to step aside. It sees itself as part of change that it still passionately believes will occur."

Consider this, then, a call to arms. More appropriately, consider it a call to the flowers that war protesters shoved down the barrels of those arms, back in the day.

Most of us are fit and financially secure. We've got our wits and a modicum of wisdom. We're weather-beaten, yes. But that means we're seasoned, too. Heck, we're more than seasoned. We're marinated. And the skills we've acquired with time are honed and at the ready.

The harebrained dream we harboured way back when is itching to be free, now. It's weak and more than a little worn. But it's breathing.

What if our dream just needs some fresh air and sunshine and a healthy injection of nutrients?

Just watch what can happen if we finally let it loose.

PART 5: The Dept. of Health And Welfare

19 Om My!

"Why they always look so serious in Yoga? You make serious face like this, you scare away good energy. To meditate, only you must smile."

— Ketut Liyer, a Balinese healer

The local community centre is offering yoga again. I thought about it for one very foolish moment. Then I remembered last summer's foray into lotus land. And I moved on.

This is me in yoga class: The legs are supposed to be crossed and the eyes are supposed to be closed. Naturally, the eyes are crossed and the legs are closed.

We've always had a rocky relationship – me and coordination – and now we've had words. We've said things we didn't mean. We've parted ways again.

In fact, coordination seems to have jilted me for good, in favour of that lithe, composed creature inevitably sitting on the mat next to mine.

But I'm determined to woo coordination back. I cross my legs and close my eyes with conviction.

Too much conviction to achieve ecstasy, but what the hey. I'm a modern woman, goal-oriented, a little, shall we say, driven.

If that soft-spoken aura-bathed angel at the front of the room instructs me to "centre," then, dagnabit, "centre" I shall.

There were about seven other such modern women doing the Downward Dog at my final yoga outing in a dimly-lit venue last year.

Most of us were pushing 60 like Sisyphus, shoving a rock all the way up some never-ending hill.

Part of a Major Boomer Trend, we were all aspiring practitioners of the 5,000-year-old exercise regimen that originated in India.

An estimated 1.4 million Canadians now include some form of yoga in their weekly routine, five times what the figure was just 10 years ago.

And because yoga goes easy on older bones and less flexible muscles, many of them fall into our age bracket.

"The influx of newcomers to yoga is phenomenal," says one yogi who conducts such classes.

"Boomers have slowed down from marathons to aerobics and from aerobics to yoga, which is kinder to the system. But the whole purpose is to become more connected and that can only be done if you withdraw and learn to be still."

In other words, calling yoga an exercise regimen does the divine practice an injustice.

Yoga is more properly defined as a system of philosophy and meditation intended to help the body and soul attain union with the universal spirit.

Oh, wait a minute. There goes my cell phone.

Is it okay to put the universal spirit on hold while I deal with a long-distance call from my kid? I guess not.

The universal spirit turns out to be a tad impatient. It appears to have hung up when I try to reconnect.

Luckily, efficient as I am, I have programmed the spirit's number into my phone after last week's session. I call back. The spirit answers. It seems a little miffed.

Who can blame it?

The universal spirit is tired of dealing with yoga dilettantes like me. I'm stressed. I'm full of angst. My synapses are bouncing off the walls.

And I've only recently learned that my "centre" is not necessarily in the place where I used to work.

Still, the universal spirit loves a challenge. That's why people are signing up in droves in desperate search of an hour-and-a-half's worth of instant enlightenment.

Now, in deference to the universal spirit, I turn off my cell, and get busy with the transcendental work of communing.

But there's this persistent itch on my left calf that simply won't let up. I need my eyes to zero in on it. Gotta send that itch packing before I can "centre."

I open my eyes, scratch, and absentmindedly scan the room. This can only be good, I reason: absence of mind is the idea, isn't it?

My colleagues in rapture are supposedly "centering" too.

I notice that the woman to my right is snoring lightly and the woman in front of me is shaking her watch.

But the angel who is leading us is a model of bliss and tranquility. She encourages us now to pound our chests and chant. "I am!" we respond dutifully. "I am, I am, I am."

A shred of flotsam interrupts my newfound serenity. "I yam what I yam and that's all that I yam," it goes.

"I'm Popeye the Sailor Man."

Nope. No yoga for me, this summer.

20 Body Bravery

"The thing about sport, any sport, is that swearing is very much part of it."

— British athlete Jimmy Greaves (b: 1940)

When they're not doing performance-enhancing drugs – for that matter, sometimes even when they are – Olympians are a fresh-faced lot. Their eyes shine, their teeth gleam, their pecs are defined. Their hair is sleek and rich and full – if they haven't shaved it off in the style of the day or for the purposes of improving their speed. They are focused, graceful, sharp and keenly competitive. They work hard and long to accomplish their record-breaking feats. They're young, carved and supple.

They are also, to someone like me, from Jupiter.

I am aging and creaky, given to wobbly parts. My inactivity is probably shaving years from my life.

Yet I'm afraid it was always thus. There are those who are born lithe and physically gifted. They have a kind of innate bravery that makes them become the first two-year-old on the block to climb the tree to its highest branch or to aim to get the swing over the top of the bar.

They are fleet and elegant in their movements from the moment they're sure on their feet.

I was the kind of kid who feared heights, speed – any physical challenge that I perceived could put me in danger. I walked tentatively from the moment I walked.

And the moment I walked is my first sharp memory – not because my memory extends back so far, but because I was such a late walker. I toddled – and the family cheered in unison, because it had been such a long time coming. You couldn't get me to climb the ladder that led to the playground slide, let alone a tree.

Another of my earliest memories was of the concussion I received in gym class. Miss Moran was my gym teacher then. I think she was bitter about her life. Her face was always pinched – and she threw balls with what seemed to me an undue force. She didn't much like those of us who were uncertain. She singled us out with stinging criticism of our movements. She was cruel, really.

We were playing some God-awful game called Red Rover. The rules escape me now, but I know it entailed all of us running wildly like the panicked populace when Godzilla was afoot. I was not fast. Somebody stepped on my heel and I went down. Hit the concrete gym floor full force.

Knocked out cold. Had my one-and-only out-of-body experience. I recall watching myself being carried to the nurse's office by a couple of teachers. I remember being transported to hospital. It was just before Christmas and I was on the neurology ward for a day and a half, along with children who were much, much sicker than I was.

I remember the guilt of leaving the hospital with an armload of Christmas gifts, which had been donated to us poor unfortunates stuck on the ward over the holidays. After all, I was Jewish. And I was fine. I still took them home, though.

I tried two sports semi-seriously in my lifetime. I was a not-bad gymnast in grade school. I had the right tiny build for it and I loved the sensation of twirling between the uneven parallel bars. Until I fell off one day and nearly fractured an arm. Ms. Moran didn't say a word. She just rolled her eyes. That was enough to discourage me.

In high school I tried fencing – and that was great fun, as long as it lasted. I loved the outfits fencers had to wear. I loved the protection the mask provided and the ramrod straight stance I had to develop. I loved it when the coach shouted "En Garde!" "Thrust!" "Lunge!" "Touché!"

In fact, it soon became clear that I loved the accoutrements much more than I loved fencing itself. After a while, I dropped it and joined the drama club.

Truth is, I just don't relate to participant sports. Never have. Never will.

No one has tried to convince me to think otherwise of myself – although several have tried to encourage me to get off my butt and take care of this remarkable vessel that holds my soul. Run, they say. Lift weights. Swim. Power walk. Build yourself up.

Yeah. One of these days. I still lack confidence in my body and what it can do for me. All these years later I should know better, but I can't get past the humiliation of being the clichéd last kid picked for the schoolyard team.

21 Sven the Improbable

"There is a fifth dimension beyond that which is known to man. It is a dimension as vast as space and as timeless as infinity. It is the middle ground between light and shadow, between science and superstition, and it lies between the pit of man's fears and the summit of his knowledge. This is the dimension of imagination. It is an area which we call the Twilight Zone."

— Rod Serling, scriptwriter and host, *The Twilight Zone*, circa 1960

And in that dimension, some 60-year-old Swede, whom we shall name Sven – a glistening he-man with a sneer – is kicking sand in the faces of Santa Claus, the Tooth Fairy and Elijah the Prophet. (The latter supposedly visits every Jewish home at Passover to have a sip of wine, which once led my then-8-year-old son Ted to muse: "I hope he's not driving...").

That's because according to a recent revelation, Sven is a fraud – a figment of Participaction, the federally sponsored fitness organization. The "average" 60-year-old Swede – that would be our Sven – was touted in the famous 1970s Participaction campaign as being fitter than the average 30-year-old Canadian. The advertisements, which ran endlessly on prime-time television, galvanized a couch-potato nation.

We haven't had a really good Royal Commission in far too long, and I suggest the time is now. This is a cover-up that leads right to the doorstep of the Queen's Canadian representative: even Roland Michener, Governor-General at the time, endorsed the campaign. Yet only now have we found out that no, Virginia, there is no 60-year-old Swede – and somebody, good Lord, should pay.

The effect this has had our country, after all, is remarkable. Just listen to this: "Canadians reacted with the biggest orgy of fitness since the Greeks invented the Olympics," wrote Hartley Steward in *Macleans* in 1977, at the campaign's peak. "Suddenly municipal tennis courts, idle for years, were jammed from dawn to dusk; the YMCA was sent reeling as a flood of fatties stormed their institutions; thousands of young executives began leaving for work an hour early with their squash racquets, and middle-aged men and women by the hundreds could be seen panting their way along city street and country lane..."

And so it became that fear of Sven was widely credited with shocking Canadians off their backsides, into the gyms and onto the jogging paths. Sven's impact may have been low-aerobic, but it was apparently also long-standing: According to a recent poll, eight in 10 Canadians admit to "exercise walking" and more than half confess to swimming at least three times a year. One in four people runs or jogs and one in five rollerblades or skateboards.

And yet. If you weren't among the hordes of earnest young perspirers who frantically began pumping iron – if you refrained from pouring your jiggly self into Spandex in order to flail your wobbly arms around in jazz-dance class – you have been living with 40 years of guilt. It's the kind of guilt, I might add, that leads directly to the leftover chocolate cream parfait in the fridge. That may be why Participaction – I sense a real conspiracy here – is still nagging us today about getting bulkier. The organization has launched another nationwide campaign, aimed at the very market it focused on last time out – the baby boomers (most of whom are closer to the mythical Sven's mythical age now than they are to 30). The fitness group claims we're getting fatter by the minute and that we can expect to put on 20 to 30 pounds between the ages of 25 and 55. In the last two decades, says Participaction, the number of obese adult women has risen to 14 per cent from just under 10 per cent. The number of obese men – 12 per cent – is up two percentage points since 1980.

I put it to you that Sven is responsible for our bad habits – and for keeping those fanatics at Participaction in weekly pay cheques. Sven was held up to us as some kind of paragon – as the personification of hardy. He was the unreachable star and we suffered because of him. We could never let ourselves dream of achieving the Zen of Sven; he stripped us of all hope. We ate to compensate. And here we are today, sitting ducks for another fitness campaign.

But I doubt they'll have the nerve to haul out Sven this time. Even if he really did exist, he'd be in his nineties, now. And I don't care how fit he might be, you just can't run a health campaign using a ninety-year-old as your poster boy.

Still, for those who fell for the scam, I suppose Sven has proven useful. There are people who even today are pedaling away on their stationary bikes, so let's give credit where due. Sven has made them what they are today – older.

22 Walking the walk

"If I'd known I was gonna live this long, I'd have taken better care of myself."

—Attributed to jazz musician Eubie Blake (1887-1983)

Spread *(v)*: To cover with a layer: *spread a cracker with butter*; To prepare (a table) for eating; To arrange (food or a meal) on a table

Middle-age spread *(n)*: Extension or enlargement as a result of all of the above

OK. OK. I know I should be making an effort to get off my duff, but – hey – I live, in British Columbia, where death from heart disease has been on the decline since 1986, according to the province's vital statistics bureau.

Cancer remains the leading cause of death here, but rates of that pernicious evil, too, have levelled off or decreased for everything but non-Hodgkins lymphoma and melanoma. The incidence of emphysema is also down, as more and more people butt out. In fact, statistics compiled in 2011 show that, with an average life expectancy of 82, we continue to walk this mortal coil quite a bit longer than other Canadians.

Reformed smokers can take well-deserved credit for some of these changes. The rest of us – and I'm looking in the mirror, now – not so much.

New and better medical practices have a lot to do with our longevity – not how we care for ourselves. In fact, all evidence suggests that even though we boomers are living longer than our parents, we're in worse health. That was the conclusion of a recent American study conducted at the West Virginia University School of Medicine and the Medical University of South Carolina – and there's no reason to believe results would be any different on this side of the 49th parallel.

The study found that boomers had more diabetes, high blood pressure and obesity than the previous generation. Nearly three-quarters of those in our age bracket had high cholesterol, compared with just 34 per cent of those who have gone before us.

And – get this – twice as many boomers were disabled and needed a cane or walker to get around.

As well, more than half said they were couch potatoes – or words to that effect – compared with just 17 per cent of the older group at the same age.

"That's an astonishing change in just one generation," said lead researcher Dana E. King. I'll say.

Consider: According to the Harvard School of Public Health, in 1979, 14 per cent of Canadian adults were obese. By 2008, 25 percent of adults were obese, and 62 per cent were overweight or obese.

Obesity is also more common among Canada's Aboriginal population than it is among other groups: Surveys from

2007-2008 found obesity rates of 25 per cent among Aboriginal groups who live off reserves, compared with 17 per cent in non-Aboriginal groups.

There is nothing to suggest obesity rates have improved since then – and they may well have gotten worse. That likely means that the incidence of cardiovascular disease will go up over the next 20 years as more people develop age-related risk factors like high blood pressure and diabetes. So what we've gained in better treatment, we're likely to give back because of our lifestyles.

Those funsters at the Heart and Stroke Foundation have more to add. In a survey, the group found that nearly 85 per cent of respondents weren't eating enough fruits and vegetables and 40 per cent didn't exercise nearly enough. One in five smoked and 11 qualified as heavy drinkers.

So much for sweet talk. If I sound like I'm hectoring, forgive me. Truly, I'm lecturing myself.

Blessed with remarkable well-being, I've been too smug for too long. How could I be at risk now? Surely, I've been far more health-conscious than my parents, who smoked and drank like mad men, ever were.

Yet over the past year, my sweet tooth has taken over my whole mouth. I seem to crave calories, and it's showing. I've watched middle-age spread form like a jelly mold around my abdomen. I convince myself that a nightly stroll around a short block with my languid mutt constitutes exercise. Turns out that being health conscious isn't the same as being healthy. I talk the talk, but I don't walk the walk. That's part of the problem, in fact. I don't walk nearly enough.

23 Aunt AGNES

"Old age ain't no place for sissies."

– American actor Bette Davis (1908 - 1989)

If you're looking for confirmation that the unyielding Ms. Davis was right, I dare you to visit AGNES on YouTube.

AGNES is the brainchild of a hilarious group of funsters at the Massachusetts Institute of Technology who work for a project called AgeLab. AGNES stands for Age Gain Now Empathy System. Not a great name for a rock group, if anyone was thinking otherwise.

Essentially, AGNES was created to simulate the physical consequences of growing old. It takes the form of an awkward, ugly get-up worn by young students, product developers, designers, engineers, marketing mavens, planners, architects and packaging engineers.

The idea is to give them a sense of what we geezers can expect to endure as our bodies break down in bits and pieces. Presumably, they can then invent devices that mitigate the damaging effects of arthritis, diabetes, deteriorating eyesight ... AGNES's ills go on and on.

"Put on this suit," says a cheery young thing who sounds about 14 in the promotional video. She's wearing a helmet with bungee cords attached to the hips to simulate spinal compression.

"You feel increased fatigue, reduced flexibility in joints and muscles and difficulty with vision and balance," she chirps.

If you can't bring yourself to watch this illuminating video, trust me – AGNES ain't pretty.

Thankfully, AGNES doesn't resemble me – at the moment. Still, as the Boy Scouts like to say, it pays to be prepared. Certainly, we have a personal responsibility to take care of ourselves and to strive for optimum health in our dotage. But our vitality may well ebb no matter what we do.

Take a long look around you and consider the city you live in, should you lose some physical capacity.

The tendency has always been for municipal officials, urban planners and economic developers to court young families.

Schools and playgrounds have traditionally received high priority in urban life. In an attempt to attract or keep budding 20-something professionals, cities boast of their vibrant nightlife.

Yet by 2032, more than 1.3 million Canadians will be over 65. It stands to reason that our communities have a responsibility to at least begin making adjustments.

Even before we approach that tipping point – and I do mean tipping point – old people are falling on cracked sidewalks and trying in vain to hightail it across intersections with lights that change too rapidly for their diminished walking speed. AGNES, with her decreased observational capacities and deteriorating reflexes, would surely stumble if she tried to race across the street, thereby breaking a hip and becoming even more infirm.

Boomers are at a cusp. Most of us are still fit and full of furious life. We want that to last. The good news: Whippersnapper planners are waking up to the fact that those of us who are getting on in years deserve better. That's reflected in the growing movement to make municipalities more senior-friendly.

The trend got a boost more than a few years back when the World Health Organization launched an initiative "to support communities in developing and strengthening health and social policies in an aging world."

WHO devised what it called A Policy Framework on Active Aging – and if you can get past the bureaucratese, it was an intriguing undertaking. The UN body solicited participation from 33 cities around the world to provide input into what they could do for their aging populations. In a nutshell, planners agree that making a city senior-friendly means just about everything from retiming crosswalks to supersizing supermarket aisles. (Bigger ones can better accommodate walkers.)

"People with cognitive decline don't leave their homes as often as younger, healthier people. [And] when they do leave, they're also much less likely to venture far," says AgeLab's Michal Isaacson. "That ... means that when you close a bank, or a supermarket, or a post office in a neighbourhood, this is a population that you're affecting."

I will fend off AGNES as long as humanly possible. But she's looming there in the not-too-distant future. The city I've chosen to live in, Victoria, B.C., has a reputation for being senior-friendly and there's every indication that it's getting onside. Let's hope the movement doesn't lose steam before we do.

24 Misty, watercolour memories

"Memory is the thing you forget with."

– Alexander Chase, American journalist and editor (b: 1926)

Where was I? Oh, yes. It's coming back to me. I was writing a screed about absent-mindedness, wasn't I? About the kind of brain freeze that results in exchanges like these:

He: "What was the movie we saw? You remember. In that place with the big ..."

She: "You mean the one with that actor, what's his name?"

He: "No. Not him. The other guy who was in the film about the mix-up. And the blond was in it, too."

She: "Oh yeah. It was terrific, wasn't it?"

It doesn't matter that he's replaying *Lethal Weapon 4* in his mind and she's grasping for an image of *Sleepless in Seattle*. The actual recollection is almost incidental.

This couple has learned to substitute the frustration of forgetting with a sort of fill-in-the-blanks consensus that gives solace in late middle age.

It's comfort enough to assume that somebody had a moment with us, once, and we enjoyed something or other together. The problem is, the feeling is less warm and fuzzy when we agree to disagree about shared events that have affected us.

He: "I still don't understand how you could embarrass me like that at the staff Christmas party in 1982. Whatever possessed you to trade tongues with Fred from accounting?"

She: "1986. And it wasn't Fred. It was George from human resources. And we did no such thing. He gave me a peck on the cheek under the mistletoe."

At times like these, how great it would be if we could outsource our memory. How helpful to be able to dial a 1-800 number and consult a customer service representative, fried grey-matter division.

Someone with a vaguely exotic voice could confirm for us, after the inevitable seven-second delay that indicates we're talking to an agent in Asia, that, no, it was Fred. The kiss wasn't on the cheek, but on primly closed lips. It did go on a little longer than propriety requires, however.

In a sense, of course, we do outsource our memories. When we're floundering around in search of the name of that book that had such a profound influence on our teenage years, there's always Google. But Google is cold and useless when it comes to conjuring up the exquisite details that are the brushstrokes of our lives.

The past refuses to stay where it's put, and that's annoying.

It's hard to adjust to the holes in the fabric of our minds. It's an affront to our pride to find that all too often names we took for granted are eluding us like butterflies in spring, that the threads of our thoughts are fraying like cheap polyester and that our favourite application on the computer is the thesaurus function. Our boomer arrogance demands better.

This wasn't supposed to happen to us. True, we might have squandered our synapses by the VW busload at Woodstock, but come on! Where was it written that we'd have to pay for it in our dotage?

It wouldn't be so bad if we didn't have all that useless flotsam bobbing around in our craniums.

Why is it that I can recite chapter and verse of that silly 1960s pop song Louie, Louie, for example – and tell you it was recorded by the Kingsmen, to boot – when I can't remember what I suddenly needed in the kitchen?

Some of us fall on studies such as one that was published in the *Journal of the American Geriatrics Society*. It was the first to show definitively that specific brain exercises can improve memory and attention in older adults.

So, we desperately turn to word games and math puzzles designed to pump steroids into the three functioning brain cells we have left. No doubt these techniques help.

But when Scrabblegram or Sudoku do get the better of us, all we are left remembering are the skills that we seem to have lost.

OK. So we aren't as quick on our feet as we once were.

We have to remember that wisdom is the consolation prize that we earn during the natural aging process, and that ... and that ... What was I saying?

25 A matter of taste

"I'm at the age where food has taken the place of sex in my life. In fact, I've just had a mirror put over my kitchen table."

– American comedian Rodney Dangerfield (November 22, 1921 – October 5, 2004)

I bet you thought you were so on trend, frequenting that chic Thai restaurant and insisting that the chef pour on the Nam Prik Pao – the secret Asian concoction that ignites a raging brush fire in your nostrils. Your palate has ripened, you think smugly. You've grown more adventurous and sophisticated with age – willing to take culinary risks, even if it means blowing your head apart.

Ha! You're on trend, all right – but it's likely no cause for celebration. I hate to be the one to tell you this, but what you are experiencing, dear 60-plus reader, is yet more physical deterioration.

According to that ultimate geezer hipster, Moses Znaimer, writing in an online edition of *Zoomer* magazine a while back, the average 30-year-old has 245 taste buds on each of the tongue's sensory bumps. By contrast, the average 70-year-old has just 88. So to compensate, duffers up the ante with spice and chili paste, hoping to shake some life into the few paltry sensual cells still holding on for dear life in their mouths.

If you're still skeptical, just take a stroll down the barbecue sauce aisles at any local supermarket. Suddenly, they're awash in items designed to cause a five-alarm blaze in your esophagus. Frank's Hot Sauce, Cholula Hot Sauce, Sambal Oelek Hot Pepper Sauce. The brands and bottles have multiplied like dust bunnies.

Coincidence? I think not. As far back as 2001, Alberta Government bureaucrats were all over this potential profit centre. In a web publication called The Aging Consumer Population, they astutely advised the food industry to market the heck out of the lumbering codger demographic. "Foods that will appeal to this age group will need to be flavor-enhanced," they recommend, adding that spices and herbs might do the trick.

Fine. We budding old biddies are used to a smidgen of condescension.

But the fine folks in Alberta didn't stop there. "Vision is not as good as it was when they were 20," they explain. "Make the print [on packaging] as large as possible. . . Make the package easier to open. [Seniors] do not always have the strength or dexterity to open pull-tabs or pull open plastic bags or even to use the can opener to open a can. . . Seniors enjoy shopping but are not able to carry heavy bags. Frozen products usually weigh less than canned product. Smaller packaging units mean less weight. Less weight means being able to carry more products." Ouch. Stop. Please.

The implicit message, of course, is that we have buying power – another indication of how boomers dominate decision-making in the boardrooms that drive the economy.

Going overboard with jalapeno pepper is just one of many ways we're changing the culture of food – just as we've changed so much in our wake. Market research shows we've got cash and time to kill. Our physical sense of taste may be on the wane, but metaphorically, not so much.

We read labels more carefully (as long as the writing is large enough). We're behind the demand for organic food, omega-3-laden eggs and the eat-local fad.

What's more, we're just beginning to do to supermarket shelves what we once did for the music business – bend it to our massive will. And as restaurants get on board, their influence will affect what we see in stores or on menus until the boom finally whimpers out.

Still, it angers me that I have just a few flavour sensors left (and 10 more pounds to show for it).

Scientists say we need whatever taste buds we have – and not just for animal pleasure.

Failure to value food could bring on starvation. And if you don't know how bad a poison tastes, you might just down enough of it to kill yourself.

It follows then, that the fewer we've got, the more at risk we are.

When it comes to the body, time, it seems, is a weapon of mass destruction.

26 Healthstyle

"Tonight's program is sponsored by pills. Red pills, blue pills, green pills, purple pills! Pills, pills and more pills! Ask your doctor if pills are right for you!"

— Caption on a recent cartoon

I have met Miles Munroe and he is me.

Miles Munroe was the hero of the 1973 Woody Allen killer comedy, *Sleeper*. He wakes up one day in the future and discovers that everything his era understood about science, diet and medicine has been debunked and reversed. In this world-to-be, cholesterol-laden butter, tar-soaked cigarettes and heaping, rich chocolate sundaes have taken on the sheen of health food. Anyone who doesn't indulge in their restorative properties is seen to be reckless.

As one of the best of Allen's earlier works, it's a sassy satire, taking succinct aim at the conviction with which we embrace the latest definitive study on this, the newest conclusive research on that. And like all good spoofery, it hits us where we live.

In this case, that's right in the core of our mortality. Allen recognized that when doctors and scientists pronounce, we want – no, need – to believe. We have an almost primal urge to get with the program – to do the One Right Thing that will stave off death for a little while longer, or that will at least improve the quality of our lives for as long as we're around. So we're willing and eager to buy into any program du jour the scientists are peddling.

Their classic white lab coats and serious expressions shout "authority." Their test tubes filled with mysterious potions intimidate us into a kind of submission. We convince ourselves that they know what they're up to.

Not to demean these professionals: most conduct their work with a genuine drive to make conditions better for us all. But all too many proofs and reproofs, recently, have recently shaken up my peace of mind.

Mammograms are the latest issue coming under scrutiny. As the debate about mammography takes on political proportions across the Western world, many of us are wondering: how often should we reasonably subject ourselves to the potentially harmful radiation associated with mammography? What's the risk-to-reward ratio?

Remember the Hormone Replacement Therapy (HRT) debate?

For at least a decade or so, menopausal women received reassurance that the treatment, said to combat night sweats, mood swings and the other discomforts that come with the winding down of the womb, was not only safe for most, but even recommended in some cases.

Purported to combat heart disease and osteoporosis, hormone patches and pills were popular with doctors, who prescribed them with some abandon.

And women slapped on these adhesives or gobbled down these tablets by the fistsful.

Then came word that the treatment can actually cause heart disease and does little if anything to prevent what used to be charmingly called Dowager's Hump.

And consider antidepressants. Talk about gobbling pills. Since its introduction in 1988, the use of Prozac or sister drugs of similar chemical make-up has grown to encompass about 10 per cent of the adult North American population.

An estimated 35 million people in the world take them. Maybe the pills are meant to unboggle the mind – but the statistics associated with them boggle it right back.

Of course, one side effect is a decreased libido. And wouldn't you know it? Out came a hot report from the labs not too long ago that says semen, taken internally in your place of choice, is good for a sad psyche.

Meanwhile, some U.S. scientists contend antidepressants work little better than sugar pills to ease the blues at any rate.

As a diligent consumer, you read all the bumph and find yourself frozen. You want to take care of yourself – you need to take care of yourself – but in whom do you place your faith? So you rush to your doctor, once again. Your doctor will know, right? Well, not really. Your doctor is just as subject to the vagaries of science as the rest of us. Still, she probably speaks with a certain command, just as she's been trained to do, and maybe you're off and running, following her advice.

The fact is, though, science is not a fixed, immutable reality. And when it comes to our health, we're as much at the mercy of fashion as are the women who haunt the Paris runways. Mr. Munroe, I'm laughing until it hurts.

27 Connections in the ether

"Whether it's by helping us search for health-related information, connecting us with doctors through online portals, or enabling us to store and retrieve our medical records online, the Internet is starting to show the promise it has to transform the way people interact with and improve their own health and wellness."

— Physician Dean Ornish, founder of the Preventive Medicine Research Institute (b: 1953)

The truth is, I didn't hit it off with Marc at first. I found him whiney – and New-Age whiney, at that. He went on at great length about shark cartilage, megavitamins and crystals, about the power of pure and positive "energy," about the healing nature of dreams. Not someone I would seek out at a party, I thought to myself. Too Left Coast.

But he was the first person I'd encountered there, and you know how it is when you're in a roomful of strangers: you bond quickly with anyone who pauses to give you the time of day.

It didn't help that this was the most uninviting "party" I'd ever attended – an on-line cancer support group. I'd found the site on the Internet after my dear big brother Lew was diagnosed in August 1998 with pancreatic cancer – a malevolent and particularly foul form of the disease that claims most people within six months of diagnosis. In the wake of the horrible news, I did what I do to make sense of the senseless: I researched. I researched my heart out, to be honest, as if I were going to be the one to find the cure that everyone – the biochemists, the geneticists, the research scholars, all the other devoted relatives – had somehow managed to miss. And that had led me to PANC-ONC (*www.acor.org/listservs/join/106*), an Internet chatline filled with bleak souls – people like Marc, from Holland, whose wife Lucy was wasting away.

Scrolling through the 30 or 40 email messages I got daily after I subscribed to the group, I began to avoid Marc, who always posted five or six of them. Time was short and I had no use for hocus-pocus, for snake-oil cures. There was nothing virtual about the desperation in his blow-by-blow accounts ("Lucy gained a pound! She seems to be responding to the powdered Echinacea!") and it made me angry because I feared what was ahead for Lew. I was also impatient with those given to "today-is-the-first-day-of-the-rest-of-your-life" aphorisms. (Well, yes. Who needs to be reminded under the circumstances?) And I had little time for people who used brackets and colons to make smiley faces at the end of their messages.

I gravitated more toward Jennifer, from San José, who sent me 45 pages of data on a treatment that was about to come online. Not to mention Elliot, from New York, whose mother was fading. He'd explored all the drug trials taking place throughout North America and posted summaries of them, with his thumbs-up or thumbs-down assessment of their worth. Didn't know him from Adam. But he wrote with such confidence and authority – with wit, elegance and knowledge – that I was inclined to trust what he had to say. It was through Elliot that I found a National Cancer Institute trial in Ottawa that looked promising for my brother – a trial Lew's own doctor knew nothing about. Forget e-commerce. For my money, this type of information exchange is the most vital use of the Net.

And I just loved Don, the leader of the group and its inspiration. He'd survived for five years with the disease, something almost unheard of. He was inevitably upbeat and full of useful information about the latest journal findings and relevant new Web sites. When Don disappeared from the group for about two weeks, you could feel people at keyboards across the world holding their breath. We were afraid to ask one another where he'd gone. And indeed, he'd had a relapse, he told us when he finally reappeared. Now, he was back in fighting trim.

Certainly, the worst aspect of this "party" was the turnover rate. When Elliot left without a proper goodbye, I knew why. He needed to mourn alone. But I missed him nonetheless. And when Marc's wife Lucy died, I found myself shocked by my own intense grief. He'd been my first friend in our sad little corner of cyberspace.

The outpouring from the list was genuine. Someone posted a letter to him. It said: "We really don't even know what Lucy looked like. I picture her as blonde, with a sharp nose and fine, long fingers." Marc, who had "talked" non-stop, never wrote back.

The trouble with virtual communities is that they can be deleted. I eventually lost my brother and left PANC-ONC myself without a word. My stranger-friends across the world had helped sustain me through a difficult period. There was a community there, for a time. But I let them disappear into the ether. I want to thank them now for being wherever "there" is.

28 To hell with two tiers

"You guys are evil. Canada's the best country in the world. We go to the doctor and we don't need to worry about paying him. But here, your whole life, you're broke because of medical bills."

— Canadian teen idol Justin Bieber (b: 1994) explaining why he won't become an American citizen

The letter sent to my brother Lew was reassuring. "We are pleased to inform you," it read – or words to that effect – "that under the terms of your policy, you are eligible to recover the full cost of the services of a registered nurse in your home for the duration of your illness."

Lew's cancer was terminal. We knew from the outset that his time was short and his condition would deteriorate. He wanted to be home with his young family in the last days of his life. But he would eventually require the kind of care that only a nurse could provide.

Up until his diagnosis, Lew had never once, in 20 years, booked off sick at work. Every pay cheque, a portion of his salary went toward health benefits, though.

Finally, it appeared, here was the miserable payoff at the end of the blackest rainbow ever.

The last thing anyone wanted was for Lew to worry about finances. Lew was hyper-responsible – the kind of guy who paid his bills the moment the postal worker slipped them through the door. He had always been anxious about money – even a little obsessive – about doing his share with his wife in providing for Benjamin, 11, and Sam, 8.

He came by his anxiety honestly enough. Our own father died when Lew was 12, back in 1960, long before Medicare. Our dad was a newsman who'd earned a respectable middle-class salary all his working life and who left behind some savings, a house with a small mortgage and a modest insurance policy.

But he'd been in and out of hospital for a good year-and-a-half before he died and his health insurance had maxed out. So the savings and the policy were tapped to pay the outstanding bills. Suddenly there were money worries. The family never quite regained its footing and Lew never forgot how it felt to watch his mother agonize when the bills came in.

Now, Lew's supplementary private insurance seemed the perfect complement to universal health care. In effect, he could avail himself of the kind of two-tiered system that many Canadians enjoy. His taxes helped pay for the basics – doctors' bills, hospitalization, chemotherapy treatment – and his insurance would cover the "frills," although the word hardly seems appropriate.

And using his situation as an example, you could extrapolate. Maybe some combination of private and public insurance – the sort of thing many reasonable Canadians would like to see happen – would be an effective way of addressing Canada's stressed-out health care system.

It simply comes down to redefining – or maybe reaffirming – what "basic" care entails, after all. No harm in reopening that discussion, certainly.

Here's the problem when you talk two tiers. The letter from Lew's insurance company arrived three days after his death.

The request for coverage had been submitted much earlier, but there had been interminable delays. Lew had had his nurse, anyway.

His wife had dug into their joint bank account and paid for the service in cash.

She hadn't told Lew, though. She didn't want him to worry.

So, in the hours before his death, when she was exchanging the kind of inanities and profundities that loving spouses do under these circumstances, she'd kept a secret from him, and it grated.

Lew's for-profit health insurance company – a reputable firm, long established – seemed to be stonewalling and stalling from the moment the request was made. Where was this form, they wanted to know, and where was that signature?

In our most cynical moments, Lew's wife and I concluded the company had been gambling that my brother would die before they okayed the nurse, that we would not hire a nurse on our own – and that they would be off the hook, therefore, for the cost. Nothing has happened since to convince us otherwise.

I'll tell you what I find grating now. I watch those damn TV commercials that cost, no doubt, hundreds of thousands of dollars, in which the federal and provincial governments point fingers at each other about health care spending.

I think about insurance companies, I think about two tiers and I tell you this: Health care is a fundamental human right. Health care must come from the public purse.

Health care is not something to be exploited and manipulated for profit.

Health care shouldn't depend on what you have in your wallet, what your insurance policy says – or even if you have a policy at all.

If universal health care in Canada was ever threatened, I'd be out there on the front lines. Because I'll tell you this, too. No insurance company is every going to play with the well-being of one of mine, ever again.

We must fix the system, keep it available to all – and get on with it.

29 Doin' it for ourselves

"All diseases run into one, old age."

— American essayist and poet Ralph Waldo Emerson (1803-1882)

But how to fix the health care system?

As governments lay down the law and the provinces grapple with lower caps on health-care transfer payments, here's a thought none of us like to entertain: Getting old won't be pretty for the millions of Canadian boomers who are reaching that threshold.

And don't we know it. A recent poll conducted by a group called Revera Incorporated found that 85 per cent of us "are not content with ... prospects for aging" and "not confident the health-care system can meet the needs of older seniors," according to a news release detailing the survey results.

Translation: We're scared – and we have every right to be.

There has been much wrangling over waiting times for operations and inefficiencies in our network of hospitals and clinics.

Of course, any way that we can eliminate wastefulness and root out profligacy is to be commended. Another poll conducted by the *Globe and Mail* found that "Canadians recognize more money isn't always the answer. Sometimes it boils down to better, more efficient management of the health-care system."

So, yes – we should find savings. But we should also continue compelling the feds to bolster our emergency rooms and surgeries with more cash. Still, it's not just a matter of dollars. It rarely is.

Here's the hard truth: The medical profession is having a difficult time keeping up with all the changes coming at them faster than a runaway train.

Every day brings new policy: Should doctors advise women of a certain age to get a mammogram or not? Should they trust the value of PSA test results on the issue of prostate cancer?

Staying on top of the latest findings is a full-time job.

There are some excellent physicians out there, to be sure. But sometimes, under pressure to process the line in the waiting room, they seek expediencies and fall back on practices that might be dated.

To make matters worse, the sickly are also at their most vulnerable – less able, perhaps, to stand up for their rights than they might be if they had all cylinders firing on full.

They tend to put their faith in healers of all sorts at a time when rigorous common sense ought to prevail.

This is true of the articulate and highly educated. Imagine how it must be for those who are new to the country and who find themselves limited by language.

So here's a modest proposal: Our aging population needs advocates.

Picture a new profession that serves the same function that lawyers do in a courtroom. In this case, however, they would champion their clients in the doctor's office.

Trained in medical research, these advocates could present the physician with detailed reports on the most recent studies.

They could hunt down legitimate trials and tests that their clients might be eligible for and ease the way toward getting them involved.

They could challenge doctors, in a respectful manner, about their approaches to treatment. They could take issues up with private insurers and monitor hospital care.

The boomers will start turning 75 in a matter of years.

I don't know about you, but I already fret about the gaps in my internal hard drive that serves as my memory bank.

And as far as I can tell, there is no biological de-frag function to help make my brain work more effectively.

I know I'm not alone. Virtually everyone I talk to in this age bracket has a wry tale to tell about some mild mental lapse.

The fact is we're going to need help negotiating our way through the aging process with dignity and grace.

We are entering our third act under lean circumstances.

We're going to need people in our corner who can fight on our behalf to ensure we're receiving the best treatment under the best of circumstances.

The Revera poll also said that senior boomers "will expect and demand – choices that matter to them."

I reiterate: We're scared – and the tough have to get going.

Creative solutions to the coming crisis in health care are called for.

It's time to brainstorm.

PART 6: HOPE I GET OLD BEFORE I DIE

30 The Lottery

"Suicide is a permanent solution to a temporary problem."
— Phil Donahue (b: 1935)

The young woman to whom you've offered a ride is giving lip. "We're gonna be late, Mom," she mumbles, rolling her eyes, worried what the day care centre will say if she picks up her own daughter after 5 p.m.

At the last minute, something – call it God, if you like – kicks in and the car turns over, thanks to the kind gentleman with battery cables who stopped to help.

The blood pressure takes a little dip. The relief is temporary. Now that the car *can* move, it's not going anywhere. It's bumper-to-bumper out there, and the clock is ticking.

The young woman is tsking and frowning, acting like it's all your fault. Nothing to be done but watch the traffic light turn from green, to yellow, to red, green, yellow, red. The whole thing has a hypnotic quality that puts you into a state of fugue.

You sit there and make use of the meditative moment to consider the three unexpected bills you received last week. You're going to have to juggle again – probably eat into savings that have been diminishing at a scary rate.

Overhead, the sky will not release the sun from its winter prison. Your lovely daughter remains sullen. Something's going on with her. Maybe her marriage is on the rocks. Did you fail her in some way?

Maybe *your* marriage is on the rocks, for that matter. All you know for certain is that there is less of life ahead of you than there is behind. Your world seems to revolve around joyless commitments – and irritating obstacles that prevent you from fulfilling them. You're feeling pretty grim and the evening is still young.

That's not my scenario that I've just described, but with a slight variation it could be.

Yet as long as I'm healthy and of sound mind – and that's key, mind you – my scenario will be never grim enough to make me cash in my chips. Unlike a former neighbor of mine: A few years back she took her own life. If she had been decrepit and terminal it might have made sense. She was neither.

She was my age – slight, freckled and funny. She wasn't a loner or a loser. She had kids who loved her with all their hearts and, judging from the standing-room-only funeral, friends who cherished her while she was breathing and who would deeply mourn her departure.

Yet at some point during her last day on earth, despair must have gripped her and sucked out the last of the remaining vitality that had been slowly leaking from her soul.

I was not terribly surprised, I guess, by the anger so many people expressed: It seemed instinctive and proper, somehow. Suicide, rightfully, scares us.

Moments of unadulterated happiness seem all too rare in the day-to-day goings-on. We all walk the fine line between hope and despair.

Some of us are aided by the right balance of chemicals in our system; some of us are not. Regardless, we're all buffeted by fate and circumstance, traveling on our own pathway until the battery gives out.

Maybe we'll find someone to help, maybe we won't. Maybe we'll get to the day care centre on time, most likely not. It can all feel overwhelming, living a game of chance.

And we all know what the odds are at the casinos.

There's an old Catskill joke, though, that bears repeating. A pious man visits his synagogue on Saturday and prays directly to the Holy One. "God," he implores, "I've been Your faithful servant all my life. I've obeyed Your commandments and conducted myself with integrity. Would it be asking too much to win the lottery?"

Of course, a week passes and nothing happens. "God," he beseeches the following Saturday. "Why do You not hear me? Have I not always honoured You, spread the glory of Your word and respected my duties?"

When the man still hasn't won a week later, he has lost all patience with his Maker. "God," he complains. "I have done all You have asked of me and it seems my reward is to be ignored by You. Why will You not let me win the lottery?" Soon enough, a stentorian voice booms down. "Meet me halfway," it says. "Buy a ticket."

Seen with a cold eye, humans appear to be a collection of impulses and electrical responses to stimuli. The traffic light turns green, yellow, red, green, yellow, red, and we react accordingly. Viewed this way, the whole experience of living can feel mechanical and senseless – an exercise in pointlessness.

But every so often you inhale a little more deeply than usual, and you catch the scent of some six-year-old's sweet and talcumed body. You get greeted at home by a slavering and adoring mutt. Your daughter laughs at your lame pun. And you find yourself meeting God halfway.

You know you'll be stuck in traffic again tomorrow. But you buy the ticket. You always buy the ticket. It's the only gamble worth taking.

31 Black humour and face goo

"I hope I die before I get old."

—The Who's Pete Townshend (b: 1946)

"I hope I get old before I die."

— John Linnell (b: 1959) and John Flansburgh (b: 1960) of the band They Might Be Giants

Don't call us old. Please. No sir, not us. Experienced, sure. Distinguished, absolutely. Wise, you bet. But in other respects, those quotes pretty much sum up two prevalent sides of boomer mentality. It appears we are all either in Pete Townshend's camp or in Linnell's and Flansburgh's.

While some of us are content to hide that grey and find ever more colourful euphemisms for, um, hyper-maturity, others, it seems, choose to check out early and beat the crowds. Recent research by sociologists Ellen Idler of Emory University and Julie Phillips of Rutgers University showed this to be the case. The duo found that, over a six-year period, there were increases in suicide of more than two per cent per year for men, and more than three per cent per year for women among the boomer cohort.

"This is a striking new trend," said demographer Phillips. "Since the 1930s and up to the 1990s, suicide rates among middle-aged people – people aged 40 to 59 – were declining or pretty stable. But after 2000, this picture changed dramatically."

Perhaps it was inevitable that many of us would favour the Pete Townshend approach (although he himself is still alive and kicking). We're the generation least prepared for the indignity of a failing body. This aging business, after all, wasn't supposed to happen.

We swaggered our way into adulthood all those years ago demanding and expecting to be forever young, following Bob Dylan's exhortations as usual. We were confident our g-g-generation would be the first to beat the odds – that we would conquer mortality just as we'd conquered propriety. In the game of life, based on sheer numbers and will power alone, surely we were the favourites. We wouldn't die because we refused to get – you know, the "o" word.

Then we began to lose a few of our star players – not dramatically, from drugs, sex or violence as we had for a decade or two, but to physical malfunctions and to the natural passage of time. Consider the difference. John Lennon died at 40 of a gunshot wound. George Harrison died at 58 of cancer.

The Grim Reaper began quietly circulating among us, even if he was wearing a tie-dyed T-shirt. He was taking no prisoners. We could learn to succumb. Or we could call our own shots.

"As children, the baby boomers were the healthiest . . . that had ever lived, due to the availability of antibiotics and vaccines," Idler says. She suggests we never prepared ourselves for the ravages of chronic diseases. Certainly, when you're young, you get sick, then you get better. But after you reach a certain point, you get "conditions." They linger for the duration.

Most of us, however, still favour the Linnell/Flansburgh approach. When we hit 40 and began lobbying for all the overtime we could get, statistics show that fearful boomers were exercising like the dickens, doing mind-sharpening crosswords, trying to shove fate out of their path with cosmetics and diets and procedures.

Now, I'm guessing we've revised our expectations. Thank God, we still prefer to hang in there. But as we come to terms with our new reality, we have various methods of coping.

My personal approach? Keep up appearances and laugh, emphasis on the latter. Here's an excerpt from the satirical newspaper The Onion. The "article" was headlined Long-Awaited Baby Boomer Die-Off to Begin Soon, Experts Say

"Our nation must steel itself for one vast, final orgy of Boomer self-obsession as we are hit with a bewildering onslaught of magazine pictorials, hardcover coffee-table books and multi-part, Motown-sound-tracked television specials looking back on the glory days of the 1960s," Clausewitz said. "But once this great, final spasm of nostalgia passes, the ravages of age will take its toll on boomer self-indulgence, and the curtain will at long last fall. . ." on this generation.

So that's my formula as I face my distinguished, wise and experienced years. Red hair dye. Black humour.

And face goo. Lots and lots of face goo.

32 Do Not Resuscitate

"There is a certain right by which we many deprive a man of life, but none by which we may deprive him of death; this is mere cruelty."

— Friedrich Nietzsche (1844 - 1900)

I went to the beach recently with several friends, one in particular known for his sardonic humour and lust for living large. He stripped to the waist, revealing a stark, three-word tattoo strategically inscribed near his heart: Do not resuscitate.

Today, he is fit and vital. But he's had two heart attacks. He's been so close to death, he bought the T-shirt, then returned it. He has no fear of dying, to hear him tell it. Moreover, he says that when his life becomes a case of seriously diminishing returns, he has every intention of taking it.

The words on his skin – and his plan to commit suicide should he deem the time right – burn directly into his wife's psyche. She loves him and is morally onside with the notion. She wants to respect his wishes, but can't bear the thought of carrying them out at his hospital bedside, come to that – or of watching him do it himself when he declares the moment right.

My former husband and I are on the other side of this bleak equation. He wants that plug firmly in its socket, even if his prognosis is hopeless. We remain good friends, yet all the same, his take on the subject concerns me. It may oblige my children and the other the people who love him to watch him suffer, possibly for a long time.

If this is an issue gaining traction, chalk it up to Gloria Taylor, the 64-year-old grandmother with Lou Gehrig's disease. Hot talk on this divisive matter is percolating everywhere since the B.C. Supreme Court ruled on June 15 that Taylor could legally seek help to die. It also granted immunity to those who would assist her.

If the decision holds up, it will trump a judgment made in 1993 when another ALS sufferer, Sue Rodriguez, forced the issue all the way to the Supreme Court of Canada. She lost that battle – the justices at the time said anyone caught helping her die could be prosecuted – but she ultimately won the war.

She killed herself with the aid of a doctor who remains anonymous to this day. That physician likely has little to worry about now. In February 2015, the Supreme Court of Canada declared that the criminal prohibition on assisting suicide is unconstitutional, although Parliament may act to overturn the ruling.

Predictably, some members of the religious community have come down hard on the justices involved. "We have been down this road many times around the world, and all the safeguards initially put in place wind up either disregarded or eventually dispensed with," declared Archbishop J. Michael Miller of Vancouver the day after the Taylor decision. "The result is euthanasia harms not only those whose lives are taken, but those responsible for taking them."

While I respect his viewpoint, it would help if he got the terminology right. Euthanasia occurs when an ailing person is dispatched because someone other than the sufferer thinks it would be a good idea. This ruling does not make such an action legal. At any rate, it will be interesting to see if shifting attitudes over the past 19 years serve to let the Supreme Court of Canada's ruling stand.

Pierre Trudeau once famously said that the government has no business in the bedrooms of the nation. It would do well to stay out of our sickrooms, too.

In the meantime, most boomers are vigorously crafting new chapters of their biographies, to borrow the metaphor from *The Economist*.

We're the healthiest generation ever to enter the early stages of our dotage. We are learning, at last, to live in the moment, joyful for the bounty that surrounds us and for the warmth of our loved ones.

Still, aging gives us a reason to stare death down as it approaches from afar along the horizon.

If we want to meet it on our own terms, we have to make our feelings known to those around us. And much as it may pain them to do so, let's hope they honour our choices, even if those choices trouble those we leave behind.

33 Costumes by Chanel – as if

"As we age, we have a new opportunity to learn the lessons of the heart so that when the film of our life is complete, the theatre erupts to shouts of 'Bravo!'"

– Paraphrase of a brochure promoting a spiritual retreat

That's pretty much how I suspect some of us imagine our lives will end. We envision a great, dramatic sequence before our personal movie winds down – what screenwriters call the third act.

Then, the music swells, the credits roll and there's one final heart-stopping moment before the screen goes dark.

The audience is in tears. Or they're shaken. Or they're laughing uncontrollably. We may be gone, but some director, somewhere, will soon be accepting an Oscar on our behalf.

Not all third acts demand pyrotechnics or melodrama. Not all call for intensity. My own seems to be a time of summation – a period when I'm trying to pull in the messy loose threads of a well-worn, stretched-out life.

But neatness only counts in grade school. Am I the only one who also secretly hopes to exit with a grand flourish, celebrated by my loved ones for my wisdom, my verve, my risk-taking?

Is that why I upended my life a couple of decades ago, leaving my job, my marriage and my city, when my third act was just kicking in for real?

Crises of faith and confidence are often attributed to our middle years. But my guess is that they really happen a few years later, when we have quite a bit more life behind us than we have in front. Consider these facts:

• Older people are more likely to divorce.

According to research conducted by two sociologists at Bowling Green State University in Ohio, of those who went through divorce in the year they studied, one in four was 50 or older. (It's probable Canadian statistics are similar.) They call it the grey divorce revolution.

Interestingly, women are driving the trend, perhaps because they are more likely these days to be financially independent of their spouses.

Nora Spinks, who heads Ottawa's Vanier Institute for the Family, provided this possible motive: "You've got more time to think about what kind of companion [you] want to have in those last 20 years of life – what kind of caregiving [do you] want to give and what do [you] want to receive," she said.

All true, but I believe there's more to it than that. We want one last heart-squeezing shot at happiness before time runs out.

• Professionally, older people are shaking it up. A recent study found that 54 per cent of baby boomers have either started a small business before retiring or are considering doing so.

What's more, about 40 per cent of workers over 65 are self-employed. Of course, some of the reasons for this trend are purely financial. Others, however, speak to a more primitive drive.

The urge to leave a legacy is a big factor, suggests one financial adviser, Wellington Holbrook. [Boomers] want to build something that is lasting," he says.

Another factor comes into play, too. Boomers are better prepared to take chances.

According to a recent survey conducted by the job site Monster.com, more than 40 per cent of us said we were ready to take risks.

By comparison, only 28 per cent of kids ages 18 to 29 were willing to jump into an unfamiliar fray.

• Boomers are on the move. I can only back this one up with anecdotes.

Several years ago, I pulled up stakes and moved from one end of the country to the other. I can name seven friends and acquaintances who have done the same thing.

Often, we did so without a clear plan – or even an obvious motivation.

We just felt the script of our lives required a new location – an exotic setting to add a hint of mystery or romance.

Call it the third-act syndrome, but something seems to be admonishing us to go out with a bang.

Our bodies may be failing us, but our spirits are pushing back, urging us to give caution a kick in the pants.

We're all going to fade to black sooner or later.

It's only human to want to do so with a little panache.

34 No way to say goodbye

"I'm more interested in the meaning of funerals and the mourning that people do. It's not a retail experience. It's an existential one."

— American writer and poet Thomas Lynch (b: 1948)

Religious occasions lend themselves to a kind of pre-fab spirituality – and that may be why I've never been drawn to conventional celebrations that call for prayer, supplication and undue solemnity.

For me, there is something oddly contradictory about publicly sanctioned moments of deep devotion. I resist being told what to feel and when to feel it.

I recognize that specific hymns or meaningful mantras can engender wellbeing in others and I also respect the value of the communal experience for those so inclined. It's just that personally, my soul doesn't respond well to Pavlov's bell.

Group worship is not my style. If I sense a need to get in touch with my Maker, I tend to do so on my own terms and under my own steam.

Okay. Let's be honest. That doesn't happen. My father died when I was 10. An uncle pronounced this terrible loss of mine "God's will." Ever since then, truth be told, I haven't bought the existence of an all-powerful entity who holds my fate in his ethereal hands.

I'd rather believe the Maker is non-existent than to have to conclude He is cruel.

Maker-shmaker is my take on this religion thing. Better to be a hardnosed pragmatist, able to deal with what you can see – and to pay little heed to that which you can't. That's the way you get the job of living done. The laundry sorted. The food on the table. The renovation supervised. The bills paid.

On two occasions since, I've been called on to deliver eulogies – one for my aged mother and one for my brother Lew, who died of cancer in his early fifties. I hope I honoured them, but it was certainly not my intention to plead their case before some heavenly jury.

Still. I've had my moments when I've connected, I think, with something beyond – and those moments have moved me profoundly.

Twenty years ago, for example, I watched a close friend die. Her name is of significance to me, but not to you. She was 33 years old, a colleague and a soulmate.

She had an acerbic wit and a healthy skeptic's view of the state of things. She also had wide blue eyes and tight blonde ringlets that fought hard against the world-weary image she tried so hard to project.

She was a budding journalist. And for the three weeks before she died, I watched her wrestle her first major story to the ground, a profile on a local woman she deeply admired. Could she be sufficiently objective, she worried. What if the words weren't quite right?

My friend was impossible to live with during this creative process. Short-tempered, angst-ridden, taut and nervous, she would close her office door and emerge several hours later with her nails bitten to the quick.

She would tentatively offer me a draft and seek my feedback. I would offer guidance and praise, always careful to couch my criticism.

She finally finished her opus and gave it to me to read on a Friday afternoon, along with a heartfelt card. "Thank you for walking with me," it said. The gushy sentiment was so out of character, it made me smile. It was the last time I saw her intact.

Her death was a brutal exercise in the random nature of the universe.

A phone call at the right moment would have saved her.

If she'd forgotten her keys or her purse and gone in search of them, she might still be walking around.

But it wasn't to be.

She was standing casually outside her apartment building, waiting for a friend to join her for lunch the following warm, dirty late-March afternoon, when she was shattered by a 200-kilogram block of ice that slid off the roof and zeroed in on her 50-kilogram frame.

For two days, doctors and nurses pumped blood into her body to no avail. On Monday, she succumbed to the injuries. I was at her side. The medical staff cried. There was an eerie beauty to the slowly flatlining heart monitor. There was a sudden vacancy to her vibrant eyes. I swear I felt her soul dissipate as I held her hand and kissed her goodbye. I still regret that she never got to see her first big story in print.

Her funeral, the community's farewell, was a surreal experience. A stranger gave her eulogy. The service was formal and constricted, so unlike the woman herself.

The tone was elevated and remote – a tone she would have challenged for sure. It was her nature to challenge. She would have felt uncomfortable in the constrained atmosphere. She would have had words to say about it all.

I have no doubt all this was a comfort to some, but it wasn't to me, not in that way.

The exercise in ritual made me want to find a corner, somewhere all alone, to have a moment with the universe.

And that's what I did.

35 A moment in time

"The lark's on the wing;

The snail's on the thorn;

God's in his Heaven –

All's right with the world!"

– Song from *Pippa Passes* by Robert Browning

A friend calculated recently that if she were to live more or less the average lifespan of a North American woman, she had 5,000 days left in her, give or take. It was, she said, a sobering thought.

Five thousand had a decidedly finite ring to it. You can count to 5,000 in about 5,000 seconds, or under two hours. You can consume 5,000 calories over a matter of several meals. Like sand through the hourglass, to quote an old soap opera, these are the days of our lives. And they seem to slip by inexorably, ever more quickly.

As we chatted, we were sitting outside on my back deck on a perfect early summer evening watching our dogs get territorial over a stuffed chipmunk toy.

A dewy wind wafted by and the local fauna were letting us know, in that slightly desperate way they have of chirping faster and faster as twilight sets in, that night would soon be descending. The sunlight was dappled through the trees like a French impressionist painting.

My friend's calculations were accurate, of course – although her focus seemed a little coldly actuarial to me.

It's true that we get a designated amount of time on this earth. And it wasn't particularly surprising that she'd spent some of that limited time trying to figure out how much of it she had left.

It takes the abrupt arrival of a brutal kind of wisdom for us to appreciate what that means – the kind of wisdom you're likely to acquire when you have a mere 5,000 days in the bank.

Those of us sensible enough to have been born in the sinfully wealthy West usually spend the first years of our lives blissfully ignorant of how precious a resource time is. Just watch your own grandkids over the summer break from school. For them, time is elastic: There's no end to the stuff. The day is at the morn – and the morning stretches for days.

Then at some moment in adulthood – maybe it's the advent of that new baby, maybe it's when we experience the death of someone we love for the first time – we all become aware of mortality.

Suddenly, we're all accountants, whether we're conscious of it or not – measuring the moments as they whiz by, trying to tally up their worth. These tend to be our most productive years. We try to cram every last second with accomplishment and personal progress.

We are primed and in our prime, fiercely, busily alive.

There's a "now-or-never" quality to the whole enterprise of life. To use the analogy of the artist, we're putting down our first rendering at this stage.

We're capturing time on canvas and we can't pause to truly assess what we see. We're not terribly concerned with brush strokes, texture or other refinements. We simply want to get our impressions down and perhaps develop a little perspective in the process.

For many of us, that stage passes too.

The kids who so infused us with a sense of responsibility get older. The death of loved ones becomes, tragically, more commonplace. Mortality moves in to the spare bedroom and familiarity with it breeds a certain kind of contentment.

This new period of life is hard fought and, in my experience, joyful.

We're no longer quite so obsessed with seizing the day. Instead, we let the day wash over us, let it seep into our being.

We look at the canvas of our lives with the eye of a seasoned artist, adding the texture that the work lacked in its early form.

Our senses, ironically on the wane, seem heightened. The trees appear in sharper relief, music seems richer and full of new tones. Gardens emit all those smells of decay and rebirth.

The feel of a friend's hug, the taste of a fine meal…God help me, I'm becoming New Age. But we're learning to live in the moment.

There is an exquisite perfection to *Song from Pippa Passes*.

Think of mid-summer in Canada, a sane and welcoming country full of possibilities.

We may feel some guilt for the excesses we enjoy.

Certainly, most of us are aging with dignity and in comfort.

 God, if you believe in the deity, appears to be in His heaven.

All's right with the world.

At the end of the day, we have a duty to embrace that notion.

PART 7: WHATEVER GETS YOU THROUGH THE NIGHT

36 To all the girls I've loved before

"Lots of people want to ride with you in the limo. What you want is someone who will take the bus with you when the limo breaks down."

— Oprah Winfrey

Within about 15 minutes, she was confiding the deeply personal details of her marriage break-up (the usual mid-life crisis scenario on his part) and of her subsequent discovery of God – an entity she'd never before taken seriously.

She was a complete stranger, the woman we'd met over Happy-Hour-ocean-at-sunset drinks on the terrace of a charming seaside cafe. This was in the sprawling brown and dusty Pacific town of Puerto Escondido, Mexico.

And I was there in search of a little R&R with my dear friend Ev, both of us staying with my dear friend Terri, who had been haranguing me for years to join her for a week or so at the villa she rented for a month there every winter.

This grey and soggy February – a particularly stressful time in my life – I finally took Terri up on it and found myself, very quickly, in that blissful state of mindlessness that comes on the heels of just enough sun, some gentle, fluorescent surf and just the right number of margaritas. (Well. Let's be totally honest here. Maybe, on occasion, one too many.) The lush bougainvillea, dropping petals into our personal swimming pool, didn't hurt none, either.

There only two or three days, we'd already been hailed like long-lost *amigas* at a cocktail party hosted by one of the winter locals, a Portuguese woman named Anna.

The event was peopled by the kind of charming eccentrics who drift their way south in the winter – like migratory birds, but without their sense of genetic mission.

There was the Irishman from Montreal who didn't bother with the niceties of propriety or small-talk. He went straight for the outrage factor. ("You're one opinionated Pole," he told Ev, who was born and bred in Canada, after she didn't quite buy his theory that Presbyterians were merely persecuted Jews of Spanish origin). And he did it with the kind of gusto that marked him as a man who not only led with his chin, he'd had it broken a few times for his efforts.

And there was the leathery-skinned sheep farmer from Northern England who uprooted himself after falling for a Canadian woman and who'd landed here by way of Toronto. Our neighbours, the Brooklyn-born Sikh (a former dentist) and his wife, both named Suba, were not in attendance.

You surround yourself with enough odd characters and you begin to realize that confused migratory birds of a feather do manage to flock together – and that I had my own bizarre personal history to account for, certainly.

Facing my eccentricities head-on, at least for the duration of the holiday, I found myself reasonably prepared to open the book of my life to any stranger who expressed a desire to turn the pages. You get down to basics in a hurry on vacation. You have nothing to lose, really. You'll likely never see any of these people again.

Ah, but Ev and Terri, that was a whole other kettle of red snappers. (If you're ever in *Puerto*, as the cognoscenti call it, I'd recommend such a kettle, for sure.) These were women I'd known about 30 and 15 years respectively – although they barely knew each other.

There was nothing instant-coffeeish about my intimacy with either of them: it was built on years of shared moments – some inane, some profound – that together form the remarkable and soothing garment of friendship.

Ev was the one who broke the news to me of my mother's death – we were both coincidentally in Montreal at the time where my mother lived, to attend a ceremony remembering Ev's own mother's death a year earlier.

Terri, my size exactly, supplied me with appropriate clothing for the funeral.

Now, in this equatorial outpost with the two of them, there was something a little unnerving about being their only link. Threesomes, as the mother of any school-age kid knows, don't always work. Someone always seems to be vying for someone else's attention. Feelings are tender, jealousies skulk in dark corners.

But the true beauty of adult female friendships is that, by nature, they seek the calm waters and the common ground.

Women talk and talk and talk; eventually they find subjects personal and intense. Within days, the three of us found ourselves singing old Crosby, Stills, Nash & Young tunes on the balcony well into the night.

There was a comfort and a familiarity in our togetherness and I felt a personal satisfaction as I watched the beginning of the bonding process between the two, even after I caught them, at one point, whispering over my own foibles – my handling of money! my smoking! – like two (forgive me Ev and Terri) old biddies.

I laughed to myself and left them to it.

Now I keep thinking about the woman who joined us for supper after Happy Hour – and how quickly we took her into the fold. She sensed she was safe with us. And she was.

Women are talented at intimacy. It's our starting point.

It's not just a nice place to visit, these gentle and deep exchanges we share. It's where we live.

37 Serving customers since 2014

"Tradition is a guide and not a jailer."

— British writer W. Somerset Maughham (1874 – 1965)

"Tradition is the illusion of permanence."

— American comedian Woody Allen (b: 1935)

I don't know precisely what it's like at your house in springtime, but in my circle, there's a linchpin religious festival that draws friends and family in.

That we will gather is a given. Beyond that, change, chiding and gentle argument are the only true certainties. Get my clan in one place for any length of time, after all, and there's bound to be debate.

The reason each year for our rambunctious get-togethers is the annual Jewish holiday known as Passover. Two ceremonies, called Seders, usher it in. Seders are lavish supper services conducted on the eve and first night of the eight-day event – and they are steeped in ritual extending back thousands of years.

The dining table is laid out with all manner of mysterious items – a bone, eggs, salt water, horseradish, greens, an apple-and-nut concoction, pieces of unleavened bread called matzo – and participants take turns explaining their significance, reciting from a book called the Haggadah. Afterwards, food ensues. Plenty of it. Course after course.

Let me say outright that when it comes to the kind of faith required by organized religion, I am seriously lapsed. I'm no deity trasher in the manner of a Christopher Hitchens or a Sam Harris. Still, I don't see much point in contemplating an afterlife. I find it hard to believe that my behaviour here will have any impact on what happens to my soul once my body turns to dust.

But I love Passover. From the moment I was a self-aware little girl, it required me to perform certain rites on cue. As the youngest child in our household, for example, it was my job to ask the Four Questions that begin the Seder so that the wise elders around me could answer them.

I was also the one sent to open the door to let in the spirit of the prophet Elijah so he could take a sip from the cup of wine left for him at the Seder table. (Elijah visits every Jewish household on Passover for a little nip of the grape. Presumably, he doesn't drive.) And my brothers and I scoured the house searching for a hidden piece of matzo. The reward for finding it? A crisp, new five-dollar bill.

There was a point, in my early twenties, when I rebelled against the whole notion of Passover. I saw the rite as superstitious nonsense that had no bearing on my life.

Then I married, had children and convention kicked in as it tends to do. But which convention prevailed? It came as a shock to learn that my then-husband and I had different

Passover customs, which we clung to and fought over in a semi-good-natured way.

Turns out, each family adapts the Seder for its own purposes – and each Haggadah has its own take on the "proper" way of conducting the sequence of events. Clearly, there was no right or wrong, so we compromised and blended our versions.

In the end, tradition is like a game of broken telephone, with elements passed on by each generation over millennia. Interpretation, misinterpretation and re-interpretation is inevitable.

The point is, however, that tradition might evolve and bend – but it prevails. And the older I get, the more I appreciate its role in my life.

There is a strange, seductive value in routines and practices that tie us to our forebears, whether or not we are true believers.

There is a comfort to the familiar recitation of prayers and invocations. It speaks to a culture that has survived the passage of time, no mean feat.

In an age of instant gratification, where immediacy is honoured, memory is outsourced to Google and businesses proudly announce they've been around for 24 months, I'll fight for my own Seder rituals. But I won't fight that hard.

I'll take my solace in the old ways whatever form they take.

And I'm glad I've passed them on to be happily mangled by my kids once they start families of their own. (And, please – would you two get on with it, already?)

38 Ode to Billy

"Dogs are not our whole life, but they make our lives whole."

— American wildlife photographer Roger Caras (1928 - 2001)

As I write, Billy lies beside me, the picture of contentment. He should be content. He's in a dog bed that retails for about $35. I scratch his ear idly and he begs for more.

We nuzzle for a moment, serotonin bouncing back and forth between us. The bond is strong.

I don't "own" Billy. We belong to each other. My mixed-breed mutt is the only living creature I brought with me when I moved to British Columbia from the East many years ago. (Cost of putting him in cargo: $50.)

Now, like his master, he is aging, occasionally crotchety and increasingly fussy about his diet. Ninety-nine-cent Alpo just won't do for him, don't you know. And after a $1,200-plus vet fee for his last bout of pancreatitis, I reluctantly concur. This 23-pound problem has a sensitive stomach, requiring a can a day of the high-class stuff. That's three dollars and change a serving. His treats – organic dried strips of duck – are "holistic," whatever that means. No wonder they cost nearly $10 a bag.

Perhaps I'm over-indulgent. If so, once again I'm on trend – because my cohort adores critters.

According to a retirement study produced by the Bank of Montreal, 49 per cent of those of us nearing or in our age bracket share our living space with an animal. That compares with about 32 per cent of the general population.

And like me, most boomers no longer feel they "own" their pets – any more than they "own" their children. The BMO research indicates that 89 per cent of those with pets consider them to be full-fledged members of the family.

There's no figure available to tell us what our age bracket spends on pets, but Canadians in general spent $993 million on kibble and canned food alone in 2010. What's more, that sum was expected to cross the billion-dollar threshold by 2015, according to an Agriculture Canada report.

Add to that the cost of toys and accessories, grooming, veterinary care, kennels – and the cost of doting on Rover becomes a significant sector in the Canadian economy.

Certainly, there's evidence of a deep affection for dogs everywhere. Take a stroll along the any off-leash area and you'll see toy poodles in saucy tartan plaid sweaters ($55-$75), disabled pooches ambulating in specialty wheelchairs ($157-$339) and bowsers sporting collars full of bling (about $17).

Yet the industry is steeling for a downturn, say some experts. They suggest pet care in Canada will keep growing over the next few years, but that growth will be relatively slow. Then, when the boomers move on, there will be fewer people to care for all those Rovers and Rexes.

What's more, there's no guarantee that Gen X, Y and the millennials will feel as warm and fuzzy about those with body fur.

"Challenges to the growth in pet ownership are likely to be mounting ... due to [an] aging Canadian population and shift in preferences among [the] younger generation," reports the market research company Euromonitor International.

Still, as Billy ages, I'll try to maintain his quality of life.

I can relate to his aches and pains – and he deserves to be comfortable. Not surprisingly, "healthcare and dietary supplements will sustain growth," says Euromonitor.

What's more, estate planners are pushing us to provide for our felines and canines. The BMO report even devoted an entire section to the matter of naming our pets in our wills.

BMO found in its survey that about one-third of us with four-legged companions already plan to make some kind of financial bequest to our pets. Maybe not the $30 million that Oprah Winfrey has promised her dogs, but you get the picture.

I love Billy. But that's where I draw the line on the part-of-the-family spectrum. If he outlives me, I'll name someone to take care of him – and leave whatever I have to my flesh and blood.

39 Sage, with a dash of Time

"There is a fountain of youth: It is your mind, your talents, the creativity you bring to your life and the lives of people you love. When you learn to tap this source, you will truly have defeated age."

— Italian actor Sophia Loren (b: 1934)

"Healthy children will not fear life if their elders have integrity enough not to fear death."

— German psychologist Erik Homburger Erikson (1902 - 1994)

The skeptic in me balks a little at bold and blanket statements like these. I want to believe them and usually I do. I flourish when I'm being most creative, or when I'm modelling vitality to a gaggle of thirsty young students still trying to shape their budding identities.

At other times, however, the bones creak in the morning and my diminished senses remind me that – let's be honest – I'm fading somewhat. Grapefruit is not quite as tart as it once was, chartreuse not as vibrant. Perhaps I'm experiencing cognitive dissonance, a state psychologists define as "having inconsistent thoughts, beliefs, or attitudes, especially as relating to behavioural decisions and attitude change."

That sounds like me, all right. I relish being wiser than I was 10 years ago, but I'm also 10 years closer to the end of the line. Let's get real. This blessed, burgeoning sagacity will eventually cost me my life.

When I feel I'm simply growing older, that's fine. After all, the term "older" is relative and leaves room for a soul to maneuver. It suggests a future.

When I feel merely old, the world is scarier. The term is pretty darn finite.

That train of thought gets a person nowhere. So I put my mood down to a case of acute January and place a phone call to Nancy Gray-Hemstock, a Victoria woman who has embraced her current stage of life. With her business partner Annie Klein, she runs a series of workshops at local churches and community centres that encourage people like me to drink from Sophia Loren's fountain of youth.

Gray-Hemstock is a certified leader in an international program called Sage-ing, founded in 2004 "to support and promote ... the philosophy of conscious aging." According to the literature, it is "a process of spiritual development that deepens self-awareness, enhances interpersonal relationships, hones communication skills and cultivates a vision of elders as mentors and wise counsel in community."

Sage-ing espouses the notion that we can live the latter half of our lives "creatively and with purpose." It encourages people to recognize and celebrate their accumulated wisdom and to find ways of passing it on to the next generation (whether they like it or not).

In its essence, according to its founder Rabbi Zalman Schachter-Shalomi, "Sage-ing is a program of spiritual growth that can empower you to add more years to your life and more life to your years."

The voice on the other end of the phone exudes the sort of calm and grace I think I'm seeking. Gray-Hemstock tells me she brings her mentoring skills to her volunteer work at a Hospice in her city.

"People who are mature in their attitudes toward an elder culture are not afraid of death. And that's one of the things we talk about in workshops – mortality. Because death doesn't frighten us, we can walk that path with somebody else."

She says she's seeing a distinct increase in the number of people seeking meaning and awareness in the latter half of their lives.

"There's an innate desire in all of us to continually learn," she says, "and to use what we've learned to better the lives of others. That's not to say we don't have loss as we age. But what can we garner from that loss? I think at this point in our evolution we're ready for a higher form of learning that comes with the aging process."

As for me, a mother-of-pearl sun is just breaking through the clouds and the gloom is lifting. The days are getting longer and I'm determined to live in the moment. No. Scratch that. The moment is all there is, whether I'm determined to live in it or not.

Maybe I'll get the hang of being a sage. Someday.

40 Cane Mutiny

"When I grow up I want to be an old woman."

– Singer-songwriter Michelle Shocked (b: 1962)

I saw one on the bus the other day. Her back was fused into a permanent S-curve and she must have weighed all of eighty-five pounds – one for approximately every year of her life.

She had a cane – an ugly metal contraption that made no bones about its purpose. It wasn't gussied up to look like a natty accessory: it was what it was, no doubt just like the woman using it.

She also had a keeper – an infinitely patient female companion in her fifties, who tried to cup her charge's elbow before the gesture was summarily swatted away. She negotiated her way imperiously down the aisle and painfully maneuvered her four-foot-nothing frame onto a bench seat, casually taking up two spots without so much as a how-do-you-do.

Then she pulled a newspaper out of a large plastic tote (the bag promoted Fred Stanley's Used Cars, or some-such), raised it to her coke-bottle-bottom glasses, and began to read serenely. "God-damn ISIS," she said to no one in particular.

In the days when we used to be more off-handed about the power of language we would have called her a crone, a biddy or, at best, a dowager if we thought that she had money. We're more sensitive now in the era of the euphemism: sometime within the last generation or two, marketing geniuses patronizingly pronounced her a "golden-ager" or a "senior," presumably to soften the blow of approaching mortality.

In purely neutral terms, though, she was an old woman – and I suspect she would have copped to that description without blinking, without fear.

When I grow up, I want to be just like her. My body may fail me in all kinds of inconvenient and humiliating ways, but I hope that my faculties will remain intact – that I'll keep my marbles and steal a few loose ones from those around me, to boot. I want to have a cane that I can rail against the dying of the light. I want to be sharp and engaged – a force, a presence, an entity to be reckoned with until the very end.

We have our models, we old women in training – examples we'd love to emulate. Jane Jacobs is one such. The fierce proponent of humane city planning didn't just push 90 – she's shoved it. She died more or less on the road while promoting her last book, *Dark Age Ahead.*

In the latest of a long line of passionate treatises, *Dark Age Ahead* took on issues such as environmental degradation, racism and the plight of the underclasses to predict a grim and waning future. Ironically it's the vigour with which she writes, her cautious optimism and her clear-headed thinking that inspires hope that the coming decades will not be as grim as she suggests. She welds together disparate ideas like a sculptor with a blow torch and the results are equally creative.

She was well on her way to being an archetypal old woman even when she was young. An intellectual of far-reaching interests, she never graduated from university. "For the first time I liked school," she says of her foreshortened university days, "and for the first time I made good marks. This was almost my undoing because after I had garnered, statistically, a certain number of credits I became the property of Barnard College at Columbia, and once I was the property of Barnard I had to take, it seemed, what Barnard wanted me to take, not what I wanted to learn. Fortunately my high school marks had been so bad that Barnard decided I could not belong to it and I was therefore allowed to continue getting an education."

One – oh, let's call her a crone: I'm sure she wouldn't mind – who grew into her old-womanhood is Dr. Ruth. In photos she looks fashionable and saucy, a broad, insouciant smile, chic glasses framing mischievous blue eyes, deep wrinkles covering a skull topped with thinning hair. Now in her late eighties, Dr. Ruth is the Julia Child of sex – a one-woman cottage industry of eroticism. She's had a TV show, international celebrity and a huge fan base. She doles out frank and funny advice on the proper use of vibrators and flavoured condoms with ease and wit, but she's not doctrinaire about the joys of the flesh. "Sex is good," she once advised, "but not as good as fresh sweet corn."

When I grow up, I want to be crusty, difficult, opinionated, oddball, out there. When I grow up I want to be an old woman. I suspect I'm getting there sooner than I think.

41 The quiet gift

"Language ... has created the word 'loneliness' to express the pain of being alone. And it has created the word 'solitude' to express the glory of being alone."

– German-American philosopher Paul Tillich (1886-1965)

Loneliness is a rich blue on the palette of the human condition. It's the poignant wail of a single clarinet. It's that moment at the kitchen table when you realize you're holding up both ends of an illusory argument.

Maybe you engage the cashier at the grocery store in a conversation that runs just a few seconds too long. Or you offer the house cleaner a cup of tea, hoping she'll stay beyond the call of duty.

It can also take the form of emotional silence in the clipped exchanges you trade with a person you loved once, who somehow still shares your bed.

I've been there, certainly, but I can't remember the last time I felt that way – even during a recent 10-year period of singledom.

So here's my thesis: Loneliness is a malady of the young. It sounds counter-intuitive, I know, but some recent information backs me up. Put this in your pipe, for instance: According to the 2013 Vital Signs Survey conducted by the Victoria Foundation, a local charity that invests in "people, projects and nonprofit organizations," 88 per cent of respondents 55 and older said they "rarely," "very rarely," or "never" felt lonely.

Granted, Robert Janus, a spokesman for the foundation, warns that you can't read too much into that figure. The 1,186 people of all ages who took the survey were self-selecting so the results don't claim to be a truly scientific sample.

Nonetheless, he says, the bigger picture starts coming into focus when the stat is coupled with another one: 90 per cent of respondents "agreed" or "strongly agreed" that they felt "supported by loving family, companions and/or friends."

Good on us, Victoria. The quality of life here for those in our age bracket is pretty darn exceptional. But while this city is uncommonly kind to geezers, more general evidence exists to support my argument, too.

Here's what I mean. A new term has been coined – Living Alone Together (LAT) – for those who consider themselves part of a committed relationship but choose to reside separately. According to Ottawa's Vanier Institute of the Family, guess who's best at maintaining this arrangement? I'm looking at you, dear reader.

True, fewer older adults pursue LAT relationships (five per cent among those aged 30 to 39 compared to two per cent among those 70 and over). But those who do, enjoy them for longer. Young LAT couples last an average of 2.3 years compared with 3.8 years among those age 40 to 49 and 7.5 years among those 60 and over.

The institute posits a reason for this. "Once LAT relationships become commonplace and are seen as a 'viable choice,' some of the stigma that older women, in particular, experience around living alone may ease," says a report it recently issued. "LAT couples are showing [that] living alone does not necessarily mean being lonely, isolated or disengaged."

That shift is telling.

Loneliness and isolation go hand in hand.

Solitude suggests you can be engaged in community while feeling free to retreat when you want. That was tougher to do in youth. The thoughts we harboured about ourselves when alone were often critical and unkind. We took the absence of some other entity as a sign of our weakness or lack of desirability.

But we know better these days. We trust our inner voice now. We're more forgiving of our own foibles. We've come to like ourselves better.

Don't get me wrong. I'm happily cohabiting these days. But I've also known the bliss of solitude – times when sheer and utter stillness has felt like a gift.

Solitude is the colour of a sunrise. It's the moment when you find yourself in the midst of an E. L. Doctorow novel, conducting a conversation with a well-drawn character. It's the second you wave goodbye to your daughter and granddaughter, grateful for the peace that ensues. It's when your partner disappears to tinker with gadgets while you putter in the garden.

You're together. You're alone. Either or. You're OK. All is well.

PART 8: WISDOM RECEIVED

42 Gimme Gimme Never Gets...

"I hate to tell you, boomers, but putting a yellow ribbon on the back of your $50,000 SUV is not sacrifice."

— James Quinn of the University of Pennsylvania's Wharton School (b: 1953)

OK. I'm sensing an attitude shift here. Looks like a lot of people believe we've been coddled for far too long. Now it appears institutions that have traditionally used markdowns and freebies to court about five-million boomer-Canadians are beginning to rethink their policies.

In other words, look for potentially smaller loot bags, come your 60th birthday. Think pebbles and raisins – not bling and baubles.

Most of us have put our money in the same institutions since Grandma deposited that first $10 in our names as a

10th-birthday gift. We've taken out car loans, mortgages, credit cards and lines of credit and have probably kicked in more towards interest than we have received.

Is recognition of our loyalty really a hardship for banks – the same banks that have dinged us over the years with service charges for ATM withdrawals and every other move we've made?

And consider this: we've probably been shopping at the same department store for the past 40 years. We're the last generation likely to be quite so reliable. Is taking away a small token really wise?

Case in point: TD Canada Trust recently altered its guidelines regarding its seniors' package. Used to be that clients in their 60s received free chequing and unlimited transactions.

Now, however, new customers in that age bracket get only a 25 per cent rebate on their geezer accounts. And where TD has gone, the other Big Four will surely follow, if they haven't already.

"I think every business is looking at boomer demographics and what kinds of products and services appeal to them," said TD's Barbara Timmins. That's corporate-speak for watch out.

Mark my words. Next on the chopping block: discounts for museums, movie theatres and restaurants. Generous breaks every senior has enjoyed from these groups until now will likely be up for grabs.

This comes at a time when statistics indicate that nearly two-thirds of all retired Canadians are still in debt. Twenty-nine per cent are in the red on their line of credit; 28 per cent owe money on their credit card; 14 per cent carry a mortgage and 13 per cent are still making loan payments.

While those figures are pretty staggering, it's also important to remember that the divide between the haves and the have-nots is yawning and ever greater.

Between 1979 and 2008, wage earners in the top one per cent saw their income increase to 18 per cent from eight per cent. Those were most boomers' peak earning years. And if you were among the lucky ones to benefit, who can blame businesses for ceasing to bend over backwards on your behalf?

What's more, while some businesses give seniors a break, they often adjust costs across the board to accommodate the differential, said Ken Wong, a marketing professor at Queens University, in a recent interview. "I'm not suggesting they raise their prices so they can offer discounts," Wong said. But he added that prices do show the effects of other costs such as advertising.

It may even be that not all baby boomers want the discounts. Let me be honest, here. Sometimes, I don't like admitting I'm a senior.

Still, the goodies that come with the territory are seducing me into confessing.

"I'm of the opinion that a lot of people will take [the discount] if you wave it in front of them," Wong said, "but they're not going to great efforts to secure it."

One area where discounts are likely to survive? Take a wild guess: pharmacies. Big chains such as Shoppers Drug Mart offer 20 per cent off regularly priced items on seniors' days.

It's not hard to figure out why. According to a company rep, Canadians over 65 fill an average of 39 prescriptions a year. That's why they're still prepared to give us a break. We'll be cash cows until we die.

As for the rest, few people like to have privileges they have come to expect abruptly discontinued – especially those folks in our fabled generation.

We grew up impossibly advantaged during boom times. We pushed so hard for social services, we didn't create a safety net. We created a trampoline.

Anticipating our needs, our leaders brought in hospital insurance, health insurance, low-cost university education, pension plans, ample old-age security benefits and more.

Every step of the way – and for every phase of our lives – we've made sure that we are well taken care of. Of course, we have tried to spread the largesse around to those who came before or after us.

But the bottom line is that boomers are like bunnies. There are just too many of us. And we are munching away at the economy, one discount at a time.

All the same, those little bonuses seem like another civil courtesy doomed to go by the wayside.

I'm comfortable enough. We can argue about government entitlements if necessary. But leave me with a sense that despite my age – actually *because* of it – I deserve acknowledgement.

I'm talking acknowledgement to the tune of 10 per cent.

Is that asking too much?

43 ... And maybe that's okay

.

"God bless our standard of living. Let's keep it that way. And we'll all have a good time."

— from the song *Have a Good Time* by Paul Simon (b: 1941)

So let's argue about those entitlements.

We were damn lucky. We baby boomers in the West spent most of our early-adult years having a good time while we dodged every economic slug.

Our kids, not so much. Many are getting shot right where it hurts. Bullet holes in the wallet are one thing. Worse still, their expectations are being lowered every day.

Their dreams, to quote another Paul Simon song, are being driven to their knees.

We whine about the prospect of old age entitlements on a diet.

In the meantime, as recently as 2013, some 17.5 per cent of young people in North America between 20 and 24 were pounding the pavement just looking for any kind of decent work, according to some estimates.

What's more, nearly half the total percentage of youths aged 15 to 24 had jobs in sales, service, retail, food services and clerical work – traditionally part-time and minimum-wage-type positions.

Worldwide stats are altogether frightening. A 2013 International Labour Organization (ILO) study reported 73 million young people were likely unemployed in 2013 – a group the ILO calls a "generation at risk."

Meanwhile, here in North America, the middle class is shrinking, leaving an ever-widening maw between the rich and the poor – and even fewer job openings for the inexperienced.

By contrast, in our own formative years, closing the gap between the haves and the have-nots was a goal within reach.

The cost of a postsecondary education was dirt cheap and bursaries were available for those who of us who couldn't afford even that pittance.

When we left school to start earning, we grew up in an era of near full employment, when we could choose from a wide range of satisfying jobs that promised advancement and long-term income security.

Back in the day, employers happily kicked in as much as they could to RRSPs and company pension plans.

Great benefits were a given, too. Treating workers well was an important recruiting device when jobs hung like the proverbial low fruit on trees.

House prices were affordable, too, grounded as they were in economic realities rather than ephemeral bubbles.

Yes, there was a major bump in interest rates in the early '80s, but that didn't last. Mortgages were generally reasonable.

Despite the occasional blip, growth was constant. Life held promise.

And what with a postwar economy on steroids, even the federal government – a far kinder, gentler institution than it is today – was looking out for its young.

Remember OFY and LIP grants? Every crazy notion – street clinics run by hippies, trailblazers staking out Canada's Continental Divide – these and other projects were likely to be funded.

And guess what? Some seemingly harebrained ideas added wealth and value to our country.

The chance to build and create also gave us precious work experience that served us well when the funding tap went dry.

Does our cohort's good fortune keep us from complaining?

Think again. Privilege is us. Fast-forward three or four decades. Sure, we groaned when the economy went south in 2008. That prompted lots of us to stay put in our positions – thereby diminishing the employment pool for those coming up behind us.

But with our mortgages likely in hand, recovery has been within easy reach. So if we're still clinging to the thought of an old-age safety net, it might be time to get real.

Many of our kids don't know what it's like to contribute – to a safety net or anything else of worth – and it's heartbreaking to watch what's happening to those we nurtured so carefully.

Their future is at stake.

Nowadays, the ones lucky enough to find work are often reduced to languishing in jobs that offer little hope.

Take a walk through any mall nowadays. Look at the blank eyes of the retail soldiers on the front line of an economy in retreat. Sense the desperation of the servers who scramble for tips.

"I have a job," said Ontarian Emily Kisch, 22, one such server who holds a bachelor's degree in communications. "Some people don't even have that."

Working alongside her are a public relations graduate and a respiratory therapist. That's a lot of cold water thrown on burning youthful ambition.

Then there are those running grow-ops. "I looked and I looked for something else," says one student I know, confidentially describing what he did last summer. "Believe me, this line of work is all I've got going."

He may be desperate, but give him credit for being entrepreneurial – and if he doesn't get busted, at least he's earning some business experience.

44 Thrift

"Money is a poor man's credit card."

—Marshall McLuhan (1911-1980)

Nowadays, not so much. It was true enough when the great scholar said it in 1971 – a period when credit was still reserved for the upper crust. Then the boomers came of age and suddenly cash was *so* yesterday.

It's instructive that economists coined the term "disposable income" in the wealthy era right after the Second World War. Those of us who grew up then disposed of it, all right, until there was nothing left in the till.

But that didn't stop us, no sir. Sure, we disdained material goods in the 1960s. Yet we were the first cohort in history to turn legal tender into plastic magic designed to tide us over when the real stuff ran dry.

Today, there are two credit cards for every Canadian adult, the majority issued to those between the ages of 45 and 65. One-third of us carry a substantial balance from month to month.

Certainly, as part of the cohort myself, I came to believe borrowing was my birthright. For years, I've been producing that platinum card on cue and dining out on it at elegant little eateries that reinforced my sense of entitlement.

Buy now, pay later. "Later" was deliciously vague.

The Mad Men who traffic in emotions have enabled me, of course. From the time we were a teeming tribe of teenyboppers who found themselves with vast amounts of fun money to spend, savvy marketers have tapped into our yearning for more and better.

They told us the world owed us a living and they've been selling us a bigger, brasher, bolder bill of goods ever since.

Shiny cars that guzzle bucks and burp out poisons. Sprawling 3,000-sq.-ft. homes equipped with every questionable gadget and gizmo a whiz-bang Silicon Valley engineer can dream up. One thousand thread-count Egyptian cotton sheets. And many of us bought into it all, on our generation's version of the installment plan.

Oops. As recent events have made painfully clear, we owe the *world* our living – and many of us will never earn enough to make good on the debt.

Turns out that behind the curtain, the Wizard of Oz has been pulling the economic levers, producing all kinds of empty special effects.

Money no longer seems tethered to gold or other tangible goods. It's an ethereal web of digits and bytes cobbled together to form derivatives, hedge funds and other mysteries we can't really fathom. It operates on the if-all-goes-well standard – and all is not going well.

The rubber hit the road in 2008 and ever since then, the gas gage has run dangerously low. Too many of us were left to pray that we'd meet the minimum payment required when the bills came due. We prayed that the job would last. We prayed that the equity in our houses would stop evaporating, that a black hole wouldn't swallow our retirement funds. We prayed. We prayed. We prayed.

For a certain breed of people, their prayers were heard: they just weren't answered in the way they'd come to expect.

Dr. Spock may have encouraged our parents to indulge our every whim, but the gods were having none of it. They gave us the financial spanking of our lives. They sent us to our rooms without our credit cards and told us we couldn't come out until we learned the value of an old-fashioned loonie.

It's a hard lesson. "Thrift comes too late," wrote the Roman Lucius Seneca, who preceded our demographic by some two millennia, "when you find it at the bottom of your purse." He had a point.

But maybe there's time to redeem ourselves (and our supermarket coupons) yet. In typical boomer manner some of us are taking the punishment and turning it into a fashion statement. The evidence is out there. The local Craigslist is awash in barter. ("I need a haircut," reads one entry. "What do you need?") We're visiting secondhand stores in record numbers these days – and not because we're dropping off last season's designer duds. We're stopping to calculate prices in the canned goods aisle. All of a sudden, frugality is us.

If anyone can make thrift the new black, it's the Woodstock generation.

45 Losing our drive

"And she'll have fun, fun, fun 'til her daddy takes the T-Bird away"

– From the 1964 song Fun Fun Fun written by Beach Boys Brian Wilson and Mike Love

Remember how it felt the day you traded in your learner's permit for a full-fledged driver's license? The glint of silver as you twisted the key until it nestled into the ignition with a heart-stopping click? The purr and rumble of the motor engaging?

Suddenly, all pistons and cylinders – yours and the car's – were firing. You adjusted your seating for maximum vision through what passed for a windshield back then.

Cranking your window down, maybe a soft spring breeze wafted in, mingling with the smell of circa-1964 vinyl.

You backed out of the driveway, your blood carbonating, careful not to run over your kid sister's bike. The road ahead was broad and uncluttered.

What were you – 17? With a couple of tonnes of rolling steel and the harnessed power of, say, 100 horses at your command? The possibilities were so vast, you didn't yet have a vocabulary for naming them.

Boy, were we a lucky generation. Among many other gifts we were allotted, we were the first to go mobile, in the old-fashioned sense of the word, well before our brains had completely formed, or our rampaging ids were held in check.

Access to the wheel of a car meant freedom. Freedom, as in freedom from – from parents, from restrictions, from childhood itself.

Now, skip ahead 40 or 50 years. The car is so ubiquitous, it has become a kind of bionic appendage, hardwired into our systems – as second nature to our well-being as our ears or our eyes.

For many people, driving is no longer fun. It's a necessity. It still represents freedom, though – freedom, as in freedom to – to get to an important appointment or to visit a friend at the other end of the city. Freedom to get out and buy that bargain offered at a far-off big-box store.

If some kind of government daddy wants to take away our cars now, just let him try.

You're not going to want to hear this, but a few of us should seriously consider voluntarily giving them up. It's one of the indignities of aging that our senses – and therefore our bionic appendages – start to fail us. When they do, we have less and less business on the road.

A StatsCan document issued a while back had some truly frightening figures to share. As of 2009, when the study was performed, 3.25 million people aged 65 and over – or three-quarters of all seniors – had a driver's license. Of that number, about 200,000 were 85 or older.

The good news: "[T]he vast majority of seniors who had a driver's license had good or very good visual and auditory capacities and cognitive abilities," the study reported.

Ready for the bad news? Some 53 per cent of seniors who said they had "serious hearing problems" still had a driver's license. What's more, 25,000 of those legally licensed folk appeared to be actively driving. Even scarier: "Among seniors who did not see well enough to read the newspaper or to recognize a friend on the other side of the street, even with glasses, 19 per cent, or 13,600, had a license. About half of this group had driven a vehicle in the previous month," the study states.

It gets worse: In 2009, about 20,000 people diagnosed with Alzheimer's or some other form of dementia had a driver's license. Of these seniors, 14,600 had driven in the month just before the survey was taken.

No equivalent to a breathalyzer exists to test geezers behind the wheel. No law on the books bans driving while old. Nor should there be one. That said, common sense ought to prevail while we still have our wits about us, perhaps in the form of a codicil to our living wills.

Come the day when I can't read a newspaper – even with my glasses on – take my car keys, please.

If I can't hear or my mind wanders away from the semi in front of me, back to the time when I first pressed the gas pedal and sailed away, confiscate 'em on site.

46 Scam Nation

"Kind Madam: My name is Prince Oku Banutu and I seek your beloved assistance. My father, the deposed Finance Minister of Nigeria ... "

— Text of an email scam

"There are some frauds so well conducted that it would be stupidity not to be deceived by them."

— English cleric and writer Charles Caleb Colton (1780-1832)

You said a mouthful, Reverend Colton – especially in light of a study to come out of the University of Iowa. Researchers there found that as people grow older, many suffer deterioration in an area of the brain called the ventromedial prefrontal cortex. That's where the human capacity for doubt lives.

"As you normally age, this is the first thing to go," reported neuroscientist Erik Asp, who led the study. "These are vulnerable populations."

Vulnerable populations. That's you and me he's talking about – and that hurts.

And there's more bad news. As our ability to be discerning weakens, we're also more likely to be sucked in to buying "legitimate" products, no matter how iffy they are. Think every two-bit K-Tel-type product "as seen on TV."

Our "caregivers," Mr. Asp asserts, should be on the lookout every step of the way for scam artists and shady advertisers who target us. He's even calling on the ad industry to develop stricter standards as a means of protecting us.

Not every fraudster is "Nigerian," by the way. There are plenty of the homegrown variety. In fact, as far back as the late 19th century, Canadian Thomas (Doc) Kelley was perfecting techniques for relieving folks of their money.

Kelley was a patent-medicine man from Leeds County, Ontario, who travelled across North America with his revival-style dog-and-pony circus between 1895 and 1931.

The show and his medical "expertise" were free; his medicines were not. But he had a talent for self-promotion and a knack for whipping a dour and flinty crowd into a froth of goodwill, blind trust and serotonin.

At any rate, much as we hate to admit it, our sitting-duck status shouldn't come as a surprise. The anecdotal evidence has been amassing for some time. The Canadian Anti-fraud Centre reports that people in their 60s are the nation's most susceptible demographic when it comes to "mass marketing fraud."

So the hard data just supports the notion that those of us who are gullible by nature will probably get even more so with age. Eventually, we'll be gleefully dispatching money to Prince Banutu of Nigeria. Or putting up the bread necessary to collect the 640 million pounds we won in that U.K. lottery we never entered. Or sending money to our nephews in Montreal to bail them out of jams. And the slap-chop device, or the blanket with arms that looks like a shroud? Bring out the credit card!

Aren't there enough indignities associated with growing older? Did we really need this added insult? Are even lifelong doubters, who, for years, honed their excrement detectors with pride, likely to become meek and silly chumps for every snake-oil salesman in their midst?

On the other hand, perhaps we ought to approach this new study with healthy skepticism – while we still have the brains to do so. Increasingly, biologists, geneticists and neurologists are finding that our systems are intricate and interconnected – and that it's limiting to look at each of our functions discretely. We are the sum total of our experiences as well as our body parts. Possibly, then, we might just be able to count on wisdom to kick in before we open our wallets.

It pays to be vigilant, of course. No one wants to be a mark or a dupe or a sap. Regardless of age, it's always wise to read the fine print, demand verification and to check ID. But who wants to add the fear of being burned to all the other limitations those with good intentions seem to want to impose on us?

As for Doc Kelly, it's reassuring to note that he plied his trade when people rarely lived past 50.

Presumably, their ventromedial prefrontal cortices were still intact. And they were conned all the same. What did those whippersnappers know?

47 How to be perfect

"Once we accept our limits, we go beyond them."

— Albert Einstein (1879 -1955)

Self-improvement is an ongoing battle of two steps forward, one step back.

In my tumultuous 20s and 30s, I was tough on myself when I made promises to my psyche that I failed to keep. That has changed with time as I've come to recognize the good news: Progress occurs in the one-step surplus, so we're moving in the right direction, however slowly.

That's why I keep making those promises. If I achieve half of them, I'm ahead of the game.

Here are my most recent:

• I will tweet or get out of the tree

Hey, I'm hip. I've had a Twitter account since the social online forum was a mere chick (that is to say, since 2008).

Problem: I still don't quite know what to do with it. I should probably be sending links to pithy sites, but in my day, hash tag was a game you played when you were under the influence.

Currently, I follow about five people and the same five people follow me.

I'd like to suggest we've been stalking each other, but in fact we seem to have little inclination to do even that, since we visit the site perhaps once every six months.

Nothing says aging so much as losing one's grasp of technology. So this year, either I'll get Twitter fit – or I'll quit and concede that I'm officially out of the loop.

• I will learn to love gravity

Not the kind of gravity that keeps you serious, but rather the kind the heartless scientist Sir Isaac Newton discovered and that seems to be pulling various parts of my body earthward.

It starts with the face – Diefenbakeresque jowls appear where there were none before – and slowly proceeds down the torso.

The peaches begin to hang low on the tree, as it were – not to get too graphic.

Sooner or later, I must admit that this is a fact of life and that aging is a gift. I resolve to accept my body as it is – later in 2019.

Hold me to this resolution after this year's bathing-suit season.

• I will partake of a healthier diet

I spent a recent vacation with a friend who is a raw foodist. She had a way of presenting alfalfa sprouts that made them look almost appetizing, sprinkled as they were with raw sunflower seeds and pumpkin husks.

She mixed me herbal concoctions and blended up some kale shakes that made me a true believer.

After, all, my friend looked about 10 years younger than her chronological age, and her skin emitted a radiance that seemed almost radioactive. I returned home determined to improve my diet – and I have. I've cut out chocolate bars.

• I will be nicer to people who waste my valuable time

I must remember that the person who keeps me on hold for 45 minutes is likely earning minimum wage and is as much a victim of a sick service system as I am.

The fact that he doesn't register the supreme irony of the automated voice that preceded him – assuring me of the importance of my call – is neither here nor there.

The fact that I have also been neither here nor there for the better part of an hour does not give me the right to swear at him profusely.

• I will pay all bills on due dates and avoid credit traps

Having spent the better part of the past decade getting my financial house in order, by now I know that I mustn't respond to the siren call of department store credit.

Yet those sales vixens at The Bay keep trying to persuade me to buy in, with offers of discounts and such if I just take time to fill out the necessary paperwork. I will remember to bring garlic, wooden stakes and crosses to prevent me from doing so.

• I will be kinder to myself when I break my resolutions

The nature of resolutions is that they are meant to be broken.

Life improves in increments, not in leaps and bounds. Mine has been doing so steadily, almost in spite of myself.

I think I'll let nature take its marvelous course.

PART 9: DIGITALIS

48 Eternal midnight

"It is the child's understanding that teaches the adults the way of the future. They're still doing it today with modern technology."

— Children's author Michael Morpurgo (b: 1943)

12:00... 12:00... 12:00... If ever there were a symbol of boomer hubris, the flashing red LED read-out of the Betamax might well be it.

Remember the early '80s? In the parlours of our elderly relatives, the clock on spanking new VCRs seemed to pulse eternal midnight.

We'd get desperate calls from the old folks, flummoxed at the prospect of programming these revolutionary television-taping machines. Frustrated but feeling cocky in our familiarity with the cutting edge, we'd mosey on down to their aid.

"Look," we'd protest. "It's easy. You push this button here, adjust the hour like so, stick in a tape – and voila! What's the problem?"

Ah, the problem. Yesterday, someone told me that the graphics on Temple Run 2 far exceed the original. A few days before that, a kid I know tried to explain to me that files encoded for streaming are often highly compressed. If the only words you got in those last two sentences are "someone," "yesterday" and "a kid," trust me. You're not alone. Lately, my internal clock has been flickering: 12:00... 12:00... 12:00... I have met the flummoxed – and it is me.

I had my first hint of what it's like to be confounded by novelty when my own kid, Ted, was still a preschooler.

I was a tender 36 when his dad and I unpacked a spiffy hot rod of a 20-meg IBM PC, tentatively plugged it in and stood back looking panicked at this wondrous contraption.

Before we'd even begun our struggle with computer-manual doublespeak, Ted had plunked himself in front of the monitor and was deep at play, using a primitive drawing program to manipulate lines, colours and squiggles with the ease of Picasso.

"Look, Mom," he said sweetly. "I made a kangaroo."

The point is not that we had a budding genius on our hands (although I'd be happy to argue that, too) but rather that he was instinctively at home with this newfangled technology. His brain was hardwired to the future. Mine was threatening to short-circuit. Thus began a vague sense of what it's like to be left in the dust.

Take a gander at any spring garage sale nowadays. Check out the bulky stereo with its quaint push buttons gathering grime, the early fax machine with its coiled wire protruding from an old-fashioned handset, the obese TV console with its archaic knobs and dials.

Most of these items are likely no more than 30 years old. Yet how quickly they've become artifacts – relics as removed from our present-day consciousness as hand-cranked gramophones or player pianos.

And the pace of change is accelerating by the nanosecond. That cell phone you bought last year? Give it a couple of months and try hawking it on the Antiques Road Show. There's no telling what you might get for it.

We're living in an exponential world. According to a YouTube video that made the rounds a few years back, the first text message was sent in 1992. Today, the number of text messages sent and received every day far exceeds the number of people on the planet.

12:00... 12:00... 12:00... It's a symbol of hubris, all right, but it's also a symbol of stasis – the point at which we begin, unaware that we're doing it, to let the promise of innovation pass us by. We feel assaulted by it all. We're overwhelmed. We get cranky. Our synapses long to atrophy, to find permanent solace in the familiar.

Change at the speed of light, so appealing and second-nature when we're in our twenties and thirties, becomes an unsettling strobe – a constant reminder that we're in a race against the clock that we have little chance of winning.

Still, it's a race worth entering.

While we may never keep pace with the young, we have wisdom on our side. We know better than to succumb to the lure of every new tweet from the latest social network or to respond to the ping of each new communications doodad that beckons us.

Time ticks away incessantly and we've learned not to waste it on too many frivolous distractions.

But if anything can vanquish age, it's curiosity.

A mind that stays receptive to the whirring intricacies of progress flourishes.

The alternative is eternal midnight.

49 Rotary phones

"Once a new technology rolls over you, if you're not part of the steamroller, you're part of the road. "

— Whole Earth Catalogue author Steward Brand (b: 1938)

I can recall another instance in which I began to feel the passage of time. Until that moment, I still thought I was ever so cool. All it took to disabuse me of the notion was an old-fashioned dial phone and a hapless kid.

It happened in 1991, shortly after I'd turned the dangerous age of 40. My son Ted was about eight when his friend Jamie came to visit after school one afternoon. The dutiful little boy tried to call home. Familiar only with pushbutton telephony but confronted with this strange rotary device, he jabbed his baby-fat fingers into the holes and left them there to languish. Then he turned to me, perplexed. "Phone's not working," he reported.

Ouch.

Nothing separates generations the way communication devices do. To wit: If you still haven't quite shaken the habit of making high-decibel long distance phone calls from your landline on Sundays or on evenings after 11 p.m., here's my guess: You are likely collecting CPP.

Who can blame you for being slow to adapt?

Back in the day, long distance was always expensive, especially during high-traffic calling when a 15-minute conversation could easily cost an hour or two of minimum wage. If you couldn't meet the rigid time constraints, chances are you devised signals to get the important message across that you were OK. Using the operator to call "collect" or "person-to-person," you likely instructed recipients on the other end not to accept the charges.

 Promptly hanging up after two rings was another signal indicating that you had things in hand.

Then there was the magic of Morse code. If you remember receiving a telegram on CNCP letterhead congratulating you on your wedding, do I have a great early-bird dinner special for you!

Kids will always show us up when it comes to digits and gadgets: the gap between early adopters and befuddled luddites is hardly novel. Consider the following anecdote about the telegraph recounted by a whippersnapper named John Murray, who operated this new-fangled means of communication in 1905:

"One day a man – in the village – handed me a sealed letter and 25 cents," he once wrote. "I tore open the envelope to count the words before transmission. [W]ith a look of terror on his face, he told me the message was meant not for me, but for the priest at St. Hyacinthe. I politely begged pardon, [told him] I had made a mistake, put the contents in a fresh envelope and readdressed it. I then gave the key a few taps

[and] told him it was all right. The message had gone. He departed with a smile - and a courteous 'merci monsieur.' Shortly after, I resurrected the message and sent it over the wire in the orthodox fashion."

The telegraph was the Internet of its era, with one major difference. It was far more expensive to use. In the 1850s, it cost roughly 85 cents to send 10 words between Hamilton and Toronto – a small fortune at the time. That led to the brusque, familiar shorthand – Bill dead stop – that we now associate with the medium.

The world has sped up since then and most boomers I know suffer from technology whiplash. All the same, we're keen to stay abreast. We're desperate to be at the vanguard. But every time we master some cutting-edge communication device or some avant-garde technique, a new one supersedes it.

Case in point: Statistics indicate that the use of email has declined in Canada over the past couple of years. According to the website Marketing Charts, email reach has substantially declined from its peak of 82 per cent in 2009.

What has taken its place? The likely culprit is the shorthand known as texting, which requires users to restrict their communications to 140 characters or less. Bandwidth is costly and Twitter is again forcing us to marshal our thoughts.

Everything old is new again. Whether communication takes the form of bandwidth or dots and dashes, economy seems to keep forcing us to consider and reconsider whether we have anything worthwhile to say. Do you copy, Kim Kardashian?

50 The demise of the ironing maiden

"The best time for planning a book is while you're doing the dishes."

— Agatha Christie, mystery novelist (1890-1976)

"What's an ironing board?" the kid asked. Her mother wanted her to retrieve one from a hotel closet and the kid was perplexed. In the kid's world, wrinkled clothing went to the dry cleaners and came back in plastic, smooth and crisp, with razor-sharp creases exactly where they're supposed to be. She'd never seen an ironing board. She couldn't get her head around something that lacked a digital display.

In my world, the kid is missing out on something. I was 10 when I learned to iron well from a tough and unforgiving aunt. To this day, I find comfort in the smell of starch on fresh linen, in the sure and rhythmic movements I make as steaming metal flattens plackets. It's a mindless task, ironing. That's the point. Ironing is my form of meditation.

Here's a convenient truth. Robotic vacuum cleaners kill dust bunnies by the warren, but they're depriving us of the thrill of the slaughter. Mechanical dishwashers quietly purify our plates, but strip us of the companionable pleasure of wiping and stacking while chatting with family and friends.

I'm no Luddite. Certain chores of yesteryear would leave me cold. Ask me to scrub laundry on a washboard and I'm outta here.

And yet. As we find more and better ways to save our sweat, we risk forfeiting humanizing rituals and essential skills. We also risk forfeiting the time for contemplation or community that rote tasks can offer.

The risk extends way beyond housework. We live in an age when the God of Shortcuts reigns. Take away a sixth-grader's calculator and ask him to figure 142 minus 16. Note the mild panic – the genuine puzzlement – that ensues. He hasn't lost the ability to subtract. He likely never had it in the first place.

We've cheated a teacher the joy of conveying knowledge and cheated a student of the chance to learn from a sage. We don't stop to think that we've denied the boy the kind of "aha!" moment that fosters confidence and encourages exploration. Human comprehension of basic arithmetic has become dispensable – another ancient wisdom facing sacrifice on the altar of expediency.

Sometimes we sacrifice crucial survival skills along the way – a concern, for example in the north. Inuit hunters used to orient themselves by understanding wind behaviour, snowdrift patterns, animal activity, tidal cycles, currents, and astronomical phenomena. Elders taught these methods to the children, a process requiring years of tutoring and apprenticeship. Throughout it all, the young absorbed the lore and traditions of the culture, along with the critical lifesaving information.

But these days, more and more Inuit hunters have come to rely on global position systems. They're losing their link to land and history and some have died when their GPS devices failed them during Arctic whiteouts.

The kid who had never ironed – the daughter of a friend – doesn't face death because she can't press a shirt. Still, she has lost a link of her own. She'll never understand the satisfaction of bringing smooth order out of chaos. She'll never connect over ironing the way I connected with my aunt.

She's at one end of the spectrum. At the other is another friend's daughter who is avidly canning her most recent backyard harvest – pickles, beets, turnip, tomatoes – and happily making wine in big jugs from neighbourhood grapes.

Any day now, I expect to learn that she's wearing calico clothing and harnessing the ox cart to make her way down urban streets to her day job as a nurse. Her eagerness to hold on to the ways of the past is endearing and encouraging. She hasn't started reading by candlelight – electricity has its advantages. She's just trying to find her own comfort zone where convenience meets tradition.

Technological advancements are a gift. Writing on a computer means never having to retype. On the other hand, having to retype forces you to order your thoughts before you sit down to compose. It's always a trade-off, isn't it?

With all the time that labour-saving devices afford us, it wouldn't hurt to ponder more deeply what we win and lose in the exchange.

51 The rise of cultural prudery

"I would be most content if my children grew up to be the kind of people who think interior decorating consists mostly of building enough bookshelves."

— American columnist Anna Quindlen (b: 1953)

He had me at *Middlesex* and it was just in the nick of time. I'd almost walked out over *Days of Future Past* because – now, don't bother fighting me on this – the Moody Blues produce cryptic, pretentious hooey. I did warm up again when I came across his copy of Stevie Wonder's *Songs in the Key of Life*. But the jury was still firmly out when I fell upon his boxed Neil Diamond set.

The occasion was our second date – a time for some hard-nosed assessment. Science confirms that great sex is in the brain, so a surreptitious perusal of his bookshelves and record collection seemed perfectly in order before that crucial, third, you know, get-together.

Conveniently, he had vanished into his kitchen to fix us a snack and I had the run of the den. His psyche was evident at every turn. The inventory I took was quick, instinctive, arrogant and almost unconscious. Malcolm Gladwell? A tad obvious. Paul Simon? Now you're talking! Carl Hiassen? Big points for a sense of the absurd! Moody Blues? Ouch and double-ouch!

What rescued the moment was the third book from the left, top shelf. It was a well-thumbed paperback of *Middlesex*, author Jeffrey Eugenides' Pulitzer Prize-winning novel about a young hermaphrodite. Bingo! I adored that book – and its presence was enough for me to consider turning a minor squeeze into a main one. It gave us an immediate bond – a talking point. We soon found other means of connecting.

We're history now, he and I, but that's not the point. The point? There's none, really. What we have here is just another bleat of maudlin codger longing – this one for a rapidly passing phase of history when people's pursuits and interests, their judgment and their style, were readily apparent in their living rooms.

I get it. I really do. I'm about to buy an e-reader myself. Books cover an entire wall of my own parlour: the thought of freeing up all that space is intoxicating. And I get downright giddy knowing I have a five-hundred-odd playlist of songs on a device that fits in the palm of my hand.

It's all very sci-fi, seductive and efficient. No wonder CD sales have taken a huge plunge in recent years.

Nor is it surprising that Amazon reports digit-lit is selling faster than traditional books, what with all their bindings and their heft.

The move from tangible cultural products to ethereal ones is clearly here to stay.

All the same, this latest transformation feels like a pity. Not a big pity in the scheme of things, granted. It's just that even if I keep my collection, in five years or so, people will be looking at books I read five years ago.

My current reading will be hidden from view. One consequence? As long our books reside in Kindles or on Clouds, as long as our records are neatly compacted into invisible digits, newcomers to our lives will remain strangers a little longer.

Surely, you say, preferences are also revealed in good conversation. Over time, perhaps. But at the beginning of a relationship, the natural tendency is to try to make a good impression. Be honest, now. Would you admit to reading *People* if a romantic mood called for *The Atlantic*?

True, some people buy books by the yard to match the colour of their décor. There are also those who fill their brick-and-mortar shelves with yards of hollowed-out ones bearing highbrow titles. But those ploys are usually as obvious as bad toupees and give us an instant negative reading on the phony in question.

And here's the strange irony of our age. You can bare your all on Facebook or upload naughty personal videos on YouTube: no one will bat the proverbial eye.

But exposing yourself via your books and records seems almost pornographic in the current era – just a little too lewd and intimate. Lurid, even.

Get used to it, I'm afraid. The days of full, frontal taste are over.

52 Scooter bling

"Growing old is mandatory; growing up is optional."

— Oakland As hitting coach Chili Davis (b: 1960)

Can you get your head around the idea of Jimmy Choo with suction cups on the soles? How about a hearing aid/earring with enough serious bling to rival a star's borrowed jewelry on Oscar night? And can you fathom a sleek and sexy mobility scooter, activated by the touch of a smartphone button, which collapses down when it's not needed?

The first two? Not so much – yet. But the scooter – at least, a prototype of it – made a dramatic appearance at a recent Tokyo Motor Show. It's called the KOBOT and while it's not quite ready for prime time, it is definitely a reflection of the shape of things to come.

Boomers, to clumsily paraphrase the poet Dylan Thomas, have no intention of going gentle into that good night. We still want to die before we get old. We're just intent on postponing the aging process as long as we can.

According to a Pew Research Center survey conducted a few years ago, among adults 65 and older, fully 60 per cent say they feel younger than their chronological age.

Phil Goodman, author of *Boomers: The Ageless Generation*, calls us adult teenagers – and the orthotic shoe fits. What all this means is that we want to flame out in style, with dignity to boot.

We take ownership of taste. At the feet of Steve Jobs, we have learned to venerate design. And as we geezers turn to prosthetics and other products to help us seize the day, they had better be cool.

Industry, you can be sure, is starting to listen. Sure, the 18-to-34 set is still beloved by marketers for their impulse purchases of new digital toys. But we have the serious spending money, and if we're getting finicky about canes and walkers, opportunity knocks for those who are paying attention. John Martin, for one. He's president of a research company in the U.S. called the Boomer Project. He says we are in a "longevity economy" and "a growing portion of our economy will be based on the behaviours, needs and desires of the 50-plus market."

And listen to marketing guru Lori Bitter, who started something called the Move Beyond Age movement. "We wanted to start a global conversation about design, with the belief that when products are designed smarter for older consumers, they function better for everyone," she writes in a blog.

"Since the launch, we have brought this message to big-box retailers, technology companies, housing developers, health-care organizations, packaged-goods companies, aging organizations and hundreds of others. Conversations range from how to 're-tool' senior products for boomers, to how to appeal to the largest demographic in today's marketplace." Translation: what manufacturers are hearing is ka-ching! And they are responding as fast as they can.

It's not just big-ticket items that are involved, either. The concept of ageless design is having an impact on many products we use every day.

Matt Thornhill, another marketing expert with The Boomer Project, cites packaging as a likely target for change. He describes an irritation we've all experienced – the "package rage" of trying to open something that has been shrink-wrapped in impenetrable plastic. Already, he points out, the Internet shopping behemoth Amazon is offering its customers delivery of goods that are free of this prison.

"The inevitability of the age shift – more older people and fewer younger people – means the future will contain more of these examples of package designs that delight older boomers, and everyone else at any age," he writes.

"The companies that figure out this future sooner are much more likely to grab market share and expand, even in a slow economy. It's no secret the ones that still make packaging an obstacle are going to suffer the consequences."

We are boomers, hear us roar. We want clean lines and utility. We want swank and we want elegance, too.

Let's face it: we're demanding snobs who barrel through the universe, altering everything we touch. Every so often, though, we get things right. If simple functionality with a dollop of chic can help us age gracefully – when we finally concede that we're aging – I'm all for it.

PART 10: AND ANOTHER THING …

53 Boomer, be gone

"Guys who once dropped acid are now downing Viagra; women who once eschewed lipstick are now getting liposuction. At the risk of feeding their narcissism, I believe it's time someone stated the simple truth: The baby boomers are the most self-centred, self-seeking, self-interested, self-absorbed, self-indulgent, self-aggrandizing generation in … history."

—Journalist and political operative Paul Begala (b: 1961)

You talkin' to me, Paul Begala? You must be. Because it's your view that in my view, nobody else exists. I certainly don't want to feed into your skewered impression of our people.

Still, I must point out that entertainment behemoths such as CNN continue to foster our narcissism. "[Boomers are] going to be around for a long, long time," a promo for one such program announced in its promotional material, sounding turned off by the prospect in spite of itself. "Life expectancy has gone up over 30 years in the last century, and it's rising about two years for every decade – so [they are] reaping a longevity bonus."

No doubt, the 30 per cent of us who make up Canadian society are glued to the tube when such programs come on.

We do like to navel-gaze, don't we? The good news? No one but boomers watches network television anymore. So gadzillions of us are likely reveling in ourselves more or less in private.

There's a name for that.

The thing is, boomers are the Toronto of generations – which is to say, everyone who isn't living in our world seems to hate us. Our parents thought our music was cacophonic and juvenile. Our kids find it treacly and unsubtle.

Here's a typical comment on that score: Blogger Tim Byron says our taste in tunes "got more and more boring as the years went on; by the mid-1990s it was the baby boomers buying big quantities of Michael Bolton and Celine Dion. "[They] seemed to give up on new music," he adds, "retreating to the warm safety of deluxe remastered 40th-anniversary editions of albums they used to own on vinyl."

OK. I'll cop to the boxed set of The Band. But Celine Dion? That's a low blow.

More than our taste in culture apparently deeply offends those who came before and after us.

In fact, we seem to get blamed for everything – and I mean *everything*. Here's a short list:

1. The economy: In an online *Atlantic* magazine article called Who Destroyed the Economy? The Case Against the Baby Boomers, Jim Tankersley wrote during the last major economic downturn:

"I love my dad fiercely ... even though he is, statistically and generationally speaking, a parasite. ... Boomers have run up incomes for the very wealthiest ... shrunk the middle class, and, via careless borrowing and reckless financial engineering, driven the economy into the worst recession in 80 years."

2. Emotional misery brought on by bad visual imagery: "Ads are getting so depressing," wrote an anonymous *National Post* reporter in an online article called Ten Reasons to Hate the Boomers.

"Turning on the television, walking down a subway platform or switching on the radio is fast becoming a collision with mortality. We are reminded daily that our sex lives will need help, our hearts will need help, everything will need help. And that our parents are still 'doing it.' Ewwwww."

And here's my personal favourite:

3. The Catholic Church sex-abuse scandal: In what came to be known as the blame Woodstock defense, a five-year study, concluded in 2011, cited some priests' poor adaptation to the turmoil of the '60s as a major reason for their propensity to abuse children:

"There's a sexual revolution, there's an increased amount of drug use, there's an increase in crime, there's an increase in things like premarital sex, in divorce," said Karen Terry, the principal investigator of the study.

"In a number of factors, there's change. And the men who are in the priesthood are affected by these social factors."

Right. No wonder Paul Begala is a self-hating boomer.

Everyone else seems to be turning on us. I'd like to say that because we're older, they won't have boomers to kick around for much longer. But it seems we're going to beat the odds.

Sometimes, truth be told, I bore myself. But not enough, apparently to stop carrying on about us.

You hold the evidence in your hands.

54 Duffers and Hooligans

*"I'd rather be dead than singing 'Satisfaction' when I'm
forty-five."*
— Mick Jagger (b: 1943)

Duffers and hooligans. The world seems to consist of them.
Webster's doesn't mince any euphemisms in defining the
former. A duffer, says the dictionary succinctly and cruelly,
is "a fogey." Brings to mind the back nine holes at that
retirement community, doesn't it? The word "hooligan"
gets only slightly more ink from the authority. The term,
says the good book, means "a street tough or rowdy." Think
tongue studs, ecstasy-fueled raves and you get the picture.

All this came to mind following a recent broadcast of the
Grammy awards – a hotbed of duffers and hooligans if ever
there was one. There were grey duffers nominated (Annie
Lennox) and newly blonded hooligans (Miley Cyrus).
Literate duffers got the nod (the late great Jesse
Winchester) as did illiterate hooligans (Kanye West).

In fact, throughout the evening, in between the never-
ending commercial breaks, the performers who hit the stage
were equal parts duffer and hooligan. They all seemed to
get along famously. It made me a little ill. If the universe
were unfolding as it should, duffers and hooligans would
never be caught dead in the presence of one another at this
or any other ceremony.

It is the purpose of the duffer to both fear and dismiss the hooligan; it is the purpose of the hooligan to both irritate and ignore the duffer. But the universe is an odd place, these days, and Grammy airtime is worth a mint in advertising dollars. If you can grab both the duffer *and* the hooligan demographic, hey, you can sell a lot of hair dye, in colours ranging from Fuscia Sparkle to Basic Blue Rinse.

In my lexicon, it all comes down to age. By and large, hooligans are young and duffers are old. And while there may be the odd youth who bypasses hooliganism altogether – for example, anyone with stock options, no matter how old, is a duffer by definition – the reverse does not apply. Duffers can't really get away with being hooligans (unless you happen to be former U.S. President Bill Clinton, or Keith Richard. They can get away with anything).

A duffer-hooligan is contradiction in terms. A duffer-hooligan hybrid tends to elicit feelings of pathos and mild embarrassment. Jack Nicholson, for instance, has not made a graceful transition from hooligan to duffer. It's hard to cling to that outlaw image when you're caught by *The Enquirer* at some drugstore having your Viagra prescription filled.

For a while, Madonna tried very hard to make her shift from hooliganism to maturity a smooth one – but in her case, it took a heck of a lot more than a cultivated British accent. In the minds of most of us, she could never be a duffer – just a randy old lady with pretensions. After all, she pretty well forced us to look at her private parts when she was a hooligan. Dignity is hard to come by after that. After a time, she gave up trying and reverted to type. She wanted to be a duffer, though – and because she's at the tail end of the boomer demographic, that's odd. Unlike our parents' generation, which saw the slow ripening of age as a badge of honour and an inevitable rite of passage, boomers do not want to go gently into dufferism. We don't much like being duffers. We prefer to think of ourselves as hooligans with paunches. But there's nothing we can do about it. Our children, who hate Bob Dylan and his ilk, know their parents are duffers in denial.

Our children, whose idea of a musical instrument is a turntable and a mixing board – electric guitars are *so* passé – may humour the geezers from time to time, but they're on to us big time. You can't be a purveyor of wisdom and a hooligan at the same time. You have to come down on one side or the other. And as soon as you make the choice of the duffer, there's no turning back. You're a duffer until you die. You can only take comfort in the knowledge that someday, your kid will be a duffer, too.

In the meantime, though, it's the hooligan's function to shake things up – and to do so under the radar of those who sanction culture. Hooligans are supposed to be subversive and wicked and to communicate in a language duffers can't possibly hope to understand.

Yet in the name of Grammy commerce duffers and hooligans have mingled unnaturally. A gay duffer (Elton John) and an anti-gay hooligan (Eminem) kiss and make up for the millions watching globally. They've become bedfellows, so to speak. It's what we duffers used to call "selling out," when we were the hooligans.

Beware, all hooligans. You know what happens when you "sell out?" You take the first of many steps down the long golfing green that ends in dufferism – and you reach a point of no return.

55 I'll show you my legacy if you show me yours

"You know, it's just one small step from legacy to lame duck."

— Bill Clinton (b: 1946)

"I want a complete set of Canucks cards," I heard a multi-freckled tyke confide to his pal a little while ago. "That'll be my legacy." Legacy. There's a loaded word if ever there was one, fraught with significance. You hear it a lot, nowadays, from politicians and entrepreneurs, artists and hockey players, architects and even kids with runny noses and scraped knees.

When it comes to world leaders, the term is bandied about with abandon. As I write, a quick Google search unearths an article from *New York* magazine in which 53 historians debate President Barack Obama's legacy. Will it be the fact the he was the country's first African-American president? That he launched Obamacare? That he went overboard on national security? And when I last took a look, the word legacy appeared in six stories in the *New York Times* in less than a month. They dealt with topics ranging from the feminist legacy of the Broadway hit *The Heidi Chronicles*, to Blackwater's legacy after security guards from that organization's firm were sentenced to long prison terms for the 2007 fatal shooting of 14 civilians in Iraq.

It isn't quite right to say we're consumed by the notion of legacy, but it does seem to loiter at the back of our brains, like a living entity impatient to become a ghost. We all want to leave a (carbon-neutral) footprint – in cement, preferably, rather than in sand. We want history to record that we've been here, to acknowledge that we made some kind of impact.

There are brick-and-mortar legacies, of course – the homes we've created and all the goods and chattels that go with the territory. There are flesh-and-blood legacies, too: our beloved children and their children. And there are professional legacies: a body of work, an invention, a host of well-treated clients. But I suspect many of us are searching for something slightly more abstract, a philosophy, perhaps, or some Famous Last Words to impart to future generations.

For boomers in particular, the quest for legacy seems especially pressing as we enter the third act of our lives. We're taking stock of the experiences we've collected and we're trying to assemble them as we would a 2,000-piece jigsaw puzzle. We hope that what we'll come up with is a cohesive, pleasing picture, suitable for framing and for passing on. It's a noble impulse, but it just might be a futile one, as well. I'm not so certain that we're in charge of our own legacies in the end. What we want to be remembered for and what we are indeed remembered for are often at odds.

Consider Thomas Midgley, who lived in the first half of the 20th century. He was the mechanical engineer and chemist responsible for adding lead to our gasoline and CFCs to our refrigerators. Hailed at the time as a world-class innovator, he ultimately left behind a great big hole in the sky. We haven't even begun to mop up after him. Not the legacy he had in mind, I suspect.

What's more, our pursuit of the 'L' word can distract us from the joys of the day-to-day. "Life," said John Lennon, "is what happens when you're making other plans." Those of us too concerned with posterity are in danger, perhaps, of missing small pleasures and new adventures in our drive to leave a lasting impression.

The raw truth is that we don't get to solve the jigsaw puzzle we're creating. It's never finished as long as we're alive and kicking. My guess is that some of history's most influential people probably didn't give a hoot about their legacies; they were too busy doing until they were done.

When Anna Mary Robertson Moses – better known as the artist Grandma Moses – died in 1961 at 101, her work late in life had made her famous. After decades spent working on farms, Moses took up art painting the age of 76 when her hands became too crippled by arthritis to hold an embroidery needle. I doubt she gave one second's thought to her legacy, although then-president John F. Kennedy characterized her as an "inspiration to the nation" after her death.

As for me, I'm downsizing my notion of my legacy. For now, it consists of advice I offer my children. If you have spare change in your pocket, give when asked. Don't question. Don't judge. And if a car needs to be let into your lane, make room. Following these instructions won't resolve global warming, granted. But it's my small bequest and I'm satisfied with it.

56 The female boomer's biological clock

"If I had known how wonderful it would be to have grandchildren, I'd have had them first."

— American journalist and advertising executive Lois Wyse (1926 – 2007)

It's scary when the alarm on your biological clock goes off at the age of 60-plus.

I keep pushing the snooze button, but to no effect. It's not one of those soothing alarms, either. You know the kind I mean – the kind that wakes you up to the sound of swooshing ocean waves or chirping birds. Uh-uh. This one is all bells, whistles and gongs.

I'm certainly not one of those miracle women, looking to have a baby in my dotage. But the urge to hold an infant against my skin seems just as real as it did when I hit my early 30s.

This time, though, I don't want an infant of my own. I want an infant once removed. I itch to be a grandparent.

The yearning feels truly hormonal. And that's a dilemma, because while I had some control over my own driving need to reproduce, I can't control my kids' urges – or non-urges – to do the same.

I'm not alone, I suspect, in this longing. If you've passed any schoolyards recently, you might have noted that older mothers – once a rare phenomenon – are now far more commonplace. According to Statistics Canada, on average women are nearly 30 when they have their first child.

In fact, mothers over the age of 45 now account for one in every 1,000 births, according to Dr. Richard Brown a Montreal obstetrician.

That's been pushing up the age when people become grandparents, too. The B.C. Council for Families reports that first-time grandparenthood is traditionally a mid-life event: Canadians often become grandparents in their late 40s or early 50s. As usual, though, boomers skew the curve. The average age of Canadian grandparents is 65. If this trend continues, grandparents could be put on an endangered-species list.

Consider: Like many people in my generation, I was a late starter, too, when it came to parenthood. What's more, I have sons but no daughters. My boys, bless them, are now 32 and 26. They might delay procreating for another decade or two. (They might decide never to procreate at all, I suppose – but that's another story.) That means I might not be expecting my first grandchild until I'm a doddering old bird in my mid-80s – if I'm still around at all.

All this might have been brought on when a close friend was watching her own daughter's belly burgeon with life. She awaited the birth of her first grandchild eagerly and his since become a doting mother-once-removed. My friend and I have always been a bit competitive. Now, I'm green with envy. I have no indication when – or if – I'll ever experience that kind of joy.

Perhaps my new biological awakening has also been stirred by the fact that I have only the vaguest memories of the two grandparents I knew.

My dad's father lived with us until he died when I was barely three. He was an importer of jewelry. My one recollection of him is sitting on his lap while he surreptitiously fed me Lifesavers, despite my parents' protests. ("This is the colour of a ruby," he'd say, feeding me a red one, "and this is the colour of an emerald," he'd add, as I popped a green one in my mouth.)

My mother's mother died when I was just 20. She was the classic grandma with a silver knot in her hair and an ever-benevolent air. She taught me how to make a daisy chain and how to cast a purl stitch. The bond was strong, but all too brief.

We have taught our kids to be independent – and to act on reason rather than impulse. Many have learned this lesson well, keeping the natural drive to repopulate in check while they find their feet in the world. And while they wait to have children, they often do a lot of calculating. Will they be retiring by the time their children are still in high school? Will they be around to watch their children marry?

They don't necessarily calculate on their own parents' behalf, though, and that's as it should be. But what do I do with my ticking biological clock? The danger is that it might run down – and me along with it – before I can ever bounce a grandkid on my knee.

57 Speak softly, no stick necessary

"Somewhere between the overly intrusive parent and the parent who forgets about us after we're out of the house is the ideally empathetic parent who recognizes the relativity of choice, the errors of his or her own way – our need to find our own way and who can stay with us at a respectful distance while we do it."

— American psychiatrist Roger Gould (b: 1935)

Oh, Roger, you're a wise man and the advice is sound. We try – we really do – to find that sweet spot with our grown-up kids, where we can be wise and caring and at just the right distance to have just the right amount of influence.

We remind ourselves that they will and must make mistakes and missteps – that their feelings will be wrung out like dish rags and their dreams worn down like a floor that needs sanding. Chances are, all the same, they will live fine and fruitful lives. But it's hard – it's damned hard – to keep that respectful distance when they will always take up so much room in our hearts.

It starts with the momentous snip of the umbilical cord in the delivery room, this business of separating from our kids in a healthy way.

A mother's fluids and cells and sinew no longer bind her children to her physically, but these naked new beings, relatively helpless and dependent, are still fiercely etched onto her psyche.

In time, parents watch their offspring take those first tentative steps onto the school bus, then to the corner store, then to the driver's license bureau, then to another city.

With each new development, we keep retreating from their view as they advance, trying so hard not to impose our longings and our expectations as they achieve autonomy. And just as we retreat, they begin to miss our protection, coming back for more parenting against their every impulse.

Most relationships with adult children are, by their very nature, fraught. It has been our job to instill values and context and to set their moral compasses to true north. We do this despite – or perhaps because – of our own disappointments and failings. We see our kids as evolution at work, taking our genes and our instincts and our hopes and refining them just a smidgen as they nudge the human condition forward.

Naturally, they have agendas of their own. We soon enough discover that you can't force a flower to grow by pulling it out of the ground. And you can't over-water or over-feed if you want the blossom to emerge in a vivid and singular manner.

The tension between adult children and their parents has likely always been there, in some form or another.

But typically, we boomers thought we had a lock on the job of rearing our progeny. We would not repeat our own parents' mistakes of limiting our kids' expectations or bending them to our will. We read guidebooks by the dozens, inhaled the advice of authorities and waited for the moment when we would turn perfectly formed and functional beings out into the world.

So it comes as a surprise to discover that these humans we've created have quirks and foibles. Some of these idiosyncrasies are strangely familiar. Others are uniquely theirs. And it is our fate to always worry about whether we have given them the equipment they need to make their way out there.

It doesn't help that "out there" seems less a friendly place these days, where good jobs are scarce and the streets are meaner than ever. But it's always something. Coping with uncertainty, too, is a mark of maturity.

Children do not come with guarantees – and I've come to fully accept that I wouldn't want them to.

Some children are emotionally messy and complex.

Others are overly confident.

But they are ever ours.

And we have to let them unfold in their own way.

58 Too much house

"Never make your home in a place. Make a home for yourself inside your own head. You'll find what you need to furnish it - memory, friends you can trust, love of learning, and other such things. That way it will go with you wherever you journey."

—American storyteller Tad Williams (b: 1957)

For many Canadians, home is synonymous with living large – literally. And that appears to be a chronic and irrevocable condition.

Not too long ago, Royal LePage released a report that's distinctively counter-intuitive. It suggests the majority of baby boomers are not ready to forgo the territory to which we apparently feel entitled. That is to say, we aren't prepared to give up the big houses we acquired, as we were moving up the ranks, in favour of a more compact dwelling to see us through our dotage. A Leger Marketing poll conducted for the study found that nearly 60 per cent of our cohort plan to remain in our current homes. And of the 40 per cent who are prepared to move, almost half intend to buy another property of equal, or – get this – even bigger size.

"This ... clearly indicates that contrary to popular belief, most boomers do not intend to downsize any time soon," said Royal LePage Real Estate CEO Phil Soper. "They love their garages and their yards."

Not to mention our guest rooms, rec rooms and mud rooms. Statistics released by the CMHC show that as we entered the 21st century, the average Canadian home had 6.3 rooms, up from 5.3 in 1961. What's more, that figure doesn't include bathrooms, hallways and rooms used for home businesses.

The increase in actual size was even more telling. New single-family units built in the 1990s, when boomers were buying in droves, were on average almost 50 per cent larger than those built between 1946 and 1960. Meanwhile, average household size dropped to 2.6 people in 2001 from 3.9 people in 1961. In fact, a British housing market analyst reported in 2002 that Canadians lived in houses with more rooms than anywhere else in the world.

Space. The final frontier. And we have been hoovering it up.

True, our obsession with rooms that can carry an echo has levelled off since 2007. The Canadian Home Builders' Association said in its most recent survey that the average new-home size had dropped to a relatively modest 1,900 square feet. That's considerably smaller than the peak of 2,300 square feet, but still wildly excessive compared with the rest of the world.

For a time, in my recent single years, I lived in half a heritage house. It was a one-bedroom unit with absolutely no closet space. The shock to the system was significant, but this was my third attempt to conduct my life in an ever-smaller area. In the process, I divested myself of a lot of extraneous belongings – dented silver teapots tarnished beyond recognition, musty 1940s novels that belonged to my parents, avocado-hued food processors that hadn't worked since the 1980s.

The term shipshape took on a new significance for me. I reveled in my new sense of personal compression. I felt efficient and clever. I did have to work from home out of my bedroom (No, not that kind of work), but I managed this existence for nearly six years without feeling deprived.

Now that I'm sharing my dwelling with another – and I am most happy to be doing so – my new ship sometimes feels vastly out of shape. We refer to our garage as the horrible room, laden as it is with stuff we can't hope to find when we need it. Still, I'm certain I could never go back. We sprawl out comfortably in our 2,000-square-foot rental. I have the luxury of an office. The upper deck offers a spectacular view.

I can't help wondering, all the same, about our collective need to expand our living-space footprint to Sasquatch proportions. What's the force driving us to make our presence felt in such a carelessly ostentatious manner? What primitive urge encourages us to want to stake an ever-larger claim?

Size, said Thomas Henry Huxley, is not grandeur. But we crave it nonetheless. No doubt another intellectual, Sigmund Freud, would have some theories to offer.

59 Escape from Big Nurse

"No matter how many communes anybody invents, the family always creeps in."

– American anthropologist Margaret Mead (1901-1978)

Sooner or later, though, houses beyond even a reasonable size are bound to become too much. It happened to Nettie.

Ah, Nettie. All 85 pounds of her were wiry, tough and snappish. She had an arch, honed wit that slid into cruelty from time to time: she wanted you to know that she was no one's idiot. She smoked like an oil refinery in China. She'd given up giving up years ago. She was 81 and no one was going to stop her now, not with the dwindling number of days she had left.

She was going blind. She was proud, but finding it harder and harder to manage on her own. She was also a handful. Her daughter – that would be me – was caring for an infant, a schoolboy and a recalcitrant husband. No room at the inn, there. Her sons? Same scene, more or less. Not a chance. A nursing home seemed the only option – but funds were low and the choices were limited.

In the end, she was inducted into the kind of facility where fluorescent lighting casts a bluish hue on shuffling people with vacant eyes and stained housecoats.

The authorities confiscated her pack of Export A's. A friend smuggled more in. Soon, she was trafficking in cigarettes. When she died, she was on the verge of being turfed out – a rebel without a view.

I think of her often as I take my first, tentative steps into dotageville – and about how much easier I've always had it than she ever did. Some of us will live longer than our partners, who might otherwise have been persuaded to care for us. Some of us have no partners at all.

Still, I just know that many people in my cohort will not tolerate living in "retirement lodges," that smell of institutional talcum powder, where Big Nurses with a little power make arbitrary rules.

As always, we are mighty in number. We are boomers. We have standards. Hear us roar. Case in point: There is some activity afoot to create new living arrangements for an aging demographic that doesn't want to suffer fools or brook condescending authority figures. The trend is called senior co-housing and an American architect, Charles Durrett, is considered the father of this movement.

Of course, forms of cooperative living have existed throughout all recorded history. This latest version seems to be driven by both practicality and sentimentality.

We may be city slickers, but something innate in us apparently longs for a village green where friends can gather, gossip and look out for one another.

At any rate, there's one model in its earliest stages in Victoria, B.C., where a group of some 30 or 40 interested parties, ranging in age from their 50s to their 80s, have been paving the way for others.

As of this writing, they've established themselves in a rural setting and are living together as they get on.

Some might have learned from experiences with communes that failed in the '60 and '70s, because they're working hard to make a go of it before they commit. They hold workshops to thrash out issues. They toss around design ideas. They explore the meaning of neighbourliness. And one thing is certain. They will buy property together, but they will not all live under one roof. They'll have – no, they'll demand – their privacy. But by pooling their resources, they'll reduce their footprint, live more economically and form an intentional community for support and friendship.

One of the driving forces behind this project is Margaret Critchlow, a York University anthropology professor with an expertise in housing co-ops who retired a few years ago and has taken on this project. Critchlow has also launched a non-profit society and a website called Canadian Senior Cohousing. "I must like what I do," she said, "because in retirement, I'm still doing it."

According to Critchlow, evidence suggests that seniors who live in co-housing arrangements often remain for up to a decade longer in their own homes. Such an enterprise rekindles the ideals of an earlier era – without the naiveté.

If there's no incense involved, I'm in.

60 Call of duty

"Insanity – a perfectly rational adjustment to an insane world."
— Scottish psychiatrist R. D. Laing (1927 – 1989)

Some people *do* take their parents in, and my friend Ellie was one of them.

She looked after her father until he died. It wasn't always easy. His conditions had scientific names – chronic bipolar depression at first, and later the vague and deeply scary term dementia. But Ellie's dad Alec was best described as dotty. That's a word that was still OK when I was growing up – and seems apt even now in Alec's case.

Cold diagnoses say nothing about the richness of a personality. "Dotty," at least, begins to tell the tale. Heck, *I* could be dotty down the road. Perhaps I am already. I might be the last to know.

Alec's version of madness was particularly gentle – the kind of giant-imaginary-rabbit dreaminess Jimmy Stewart's character exhibited in that old movie, *Harvey*. He could fantasize about inheritances in such florid detail that he could win over staid and dour bank managers. (He nearly convinced someone who should have known better to spot him a loan because $387,046.29 would be on its way, as soon as the will was probated.) He invented marriages for friends and relatives – and did so with such authority that Aunt Lilly, huffy about having been left off one "invitation list," once actually couriered an unsuspecting couple a teapot and a snotty note of congratulations.

Over time, as his condition deteriorated, he became a handful for Ellie, his only daughter. When he lost his business, she took him in. It wasn't much fun having dad, often a giggle but intermittently depressed, camping out in the spare room. It put a strain on her marriage; it cramped the couple's style. But she never shirked her duty and he stayed until he died. He was hers. She loved him. Somehow she made it work.

Today we regard Ellie as exceptional. She used to be the norm. In the old days there was lots of support for efforts like hers. At the turn of the last century, before psychiatry was recognized as legitimate, there was always an "Alec" – someone with one kind of mental disability or another – in towns, villages and neighbourhoods.

I think of that period as one of dawning enlightenment – a time when hellish insane asylums were shut down and boarded up. In my take on it, that era had truly bad aspects, without question. People deemed strange were often abused by their families and laughed at by their peers. Then there was the language we used back then to describe people with mental disorders. "Dotty" might have a sweet ring to it, but other words were far more demeaning and vulgar: crazy, retarded, a moron.

Perhaps I'm fantasizing conditions that never were. Still, I can't help feeling that the best part of the era was the notion of kinship. While the term "idiot" is dreadful, the word "village" isn't. It suggests a sense of ownership and propriety. The community, for better or worse, nurtured each person within its fold, seamlessly incorporating the eccentrics into the goings-on. On some level everyone understood that unconventional behaviour added texture, depth, heartache and humour to life.

Many people like Alec are out on the streets these days. Hospital cutbacks mean there's no longer any room at the inn. They're being released into a lean and hungry world, one in which their co-citizens don't have much time for them.

Those on the right will say we have to rebuild local, private structures to ease their re-entry – strengthen church groups or make it possible for people to stay home and volunteer, for example. There's merit to that argument, of course.

Those on the left will tell you we have to rebuild the health system, and that's true as well. The debate will continue, while too many eccentrics sleep in doorways – and we avoid their eyes.

As we age, it's natural to fear that an "Alec" lurks inside us: there but for some mysterious grace go I. If dementia does happen, money will protect some of us. Others could find themselves fending off the elements, troubled and alone.

In the meantime, the Ellies of the world, who selflessly take care of their own despite limited resources, exhibit the kind of grace and dignity that gives you confidence in the human race.

PART 11: WHAT IS THIS THING CALLED LOVE?

Author's note: The last of these pieces were written over the course of several years, when, as a new divorcee, I explored the world of dating, relationships and love. While I've updated and changed some of the other essays in this collection, I've left these more or less intact in order to give an unvarnished flavour of the experience.

61 Love, as it looks from afar

"Still crazy after all these years ..."

— Paul Simon

I didn't mean to eavesdrop – and I didn't have to, really. I caught a few key words that told me all I needed to know. The couple were in their mid-20s, their expressions fierce. She threw down the word "relationship" like a gauntlet. He countered, fingers mauling the cup that held his latte, with "compromise." He glowered. She met his glower and raised him a scowl.

The fight was off and running.

To their immediate right was another twosome who looked to be in their early 60s. He was engrossed in the sports section while she fretted over the daily crossword. At one point, she nonchalantly reached into her purse, extracted a pill case and thrust a handful of tablets at him.

"Take these," she said, in a voice that brooked no discussion. He held her eyes for a moment, grumbled, and did as he was told.

The contrast was sharp and instructive. Couple No. 1 was in the throes of a pheromone tornado. Their conversation held a tale of torment, betrayal, desire – the whole catastrophe. Later that night he would escape their tiny apartment, slamming the door hard enough to make the hinges squeal. His buddies would commiserate as he nursed his wounds over a few beers.

On the other hand, he and his sulking girlfriend might crawl off to the respective corners of their metaphorical boxing ring. Eventually, they might begin to circle each other in the kind of seductive dance that ends up in a gloriously tussled bed – and in babies.

Now, let's follow couple No. 2. Back in their well-appointed condo, he's on the couch, nodding off, the latest Michael Connally novel lying open on his lap; she's refinishing an oak table. After a time, she nudges him gently and they turn out the lights. In bed they spoon, familiar flesh against familiar flesh, trading the inanities and profundities of the day before they tacitly agree to silence. He nuzzles her neck – an old habit that helps him fall asleep. In a matter of moments, she's breathing evenly.

On the other hand, tangled sheets are not strictly the purview of the young. Perhaps this night, couple No. 2 cups each other in places that haven't been cupped in a while: Some old longing has awakened them. Who knows why?

In our 20s and 30s, the twinkle in the eye of a potential mate is directly hardwired to organs that have nothing whatsoever to do with clear vision. We're drawn to the opposite sex by mysterious forces evidently beyond our control. In the battle between brains and musk, musk always wins.

Our job then is to make each other crazy – to test, to test and to test again, if only to ensure we can count on this person to remain at our side over the long haul. Call it a vestige of our hunter-gatherer days, when loyalty was an aid to survival of the species, but there it is.

Ah, sex and the 60s. Age is a reliable balm for burning love, for those of us who have endured the fire. Ebbing hormones make friends of men and women. Generally speaking, once we've put the reproductive drive into park, we find we can finally dispense with the hormonal equivalent of road rage. We wallow in companionship. We cherish constancy. And when we occasionally turn to each other in the dark, it's a deep, habitual intimacy that twirls our limbs together.

Still, I can't help feeling a vague sense of loss when I consider couple No. 1. No one ever wrote a love sonnet about compatibility.

I know, I know. For many of us, agony and desire are bound together in one heck of a complex knot. We disentangle them, carefully and wisely over time. The risk that intensity gets lost in the fray is an acceptable one.

Yet we all know older couples who still shoot sparks at each other like shorting toasters, but have managed to banish the misery that often goes with over-the-top love. Imagine all that passion without any of the angst.

In my view, bless them. They've hit the emotional jackpot.

62 Shotgun wedding

"There's only one way to have a happy marriage and as soon as I learn what it is I'll get married again."

— American actor and director Clint Eastwood (1930 -)

"A second marriage is the triumph of hope over experience."
— British author Samuel Johnson (1709-1784)

Forty-three years ago, a close friend had a shotgun wedding. Propriety – not pregnancy – cocked the trigger.

She was a child of 21. The previous Summer of Love had left a faint trace of erotic promise in the air.

She was ripe and she was ready.

We were all fools for pheromones back then, but the sexual revolution was in its infancy and only a few girls at the vanguard were brave enough to shack up. My friend wasn't one of them.

Her boyfriend met all the right criteria. Class? Check! Religion? Check! Prospects? Check!

Their parents were nudging them toward the altar.

In short order, there went the bride.

"I arranged my own marriage," she often says now, ruefully.

The union seemed off even before the duplicate toaster was returned. But the couple played at adulthood and soldiered on.

After the arrival of their kids, the role took hold. Several moves and a few careers later, 25 years had dissolved like a bad movie flashback.

The marriage limped along for another five years before they threw in the monogrammed towel.

Typically, the two didn't talk much about the divorce they found themselves negotiating. The parting was exactly as amicable as the marriage. No *sturm*. No *drang*. Not too many recriminations. No passion.

A few years ago, my friend, now 67, got married again. She tried – and sometimes failed – not to sound defensive when she told those around her of her engagement at the time.

 She'd been living with the man in question for three years. They're both healthy and financially stable. There was no practical reason for this gesture.

Friends wanted to know what was prompting them to make it legal. People made a point of asking, often with some distaste – as though wedding plans at that point were unseemly, inappropriate, not quite respectable.

This time around, the shotgun of propriety seems firmly aimed at the officiator.

"We just want to celebrate our happiness," my friend offers, by way of explanation, but the answer doesn't seem to satisfy.

Perhaps that's because increasingly, many of us are partnering up without benefit of clergy.

For our cohort, ever fashion-forward, marriage is *so* yesterday. According to Statistics Canada: "although the greatest proportion of people in common-law unions is under 30, in recent years, older age groups have experienced the most rapid growth. The numbers show that the fastest pace of all age groups has been among people aged 60 to 64."

Apparently people our age "don't need no piece of paper from the city hall keepin' us tied and true," to quote Joni Mitchell. Of course we don't, but for the about-to-be-newlyweds, that's not the point.

My friend's first marriage might have lasted for three decades, but it happened hastily and ended up feeling about as empty as McDonald's takeout, devoid of emotional nutrients.

Now, she's reveling in her spouse-to-be.

From the outside, their relationship looks like the equivalent of slow food. They're savouring every bite of it, taking their time exploring it and giving it the status they believe it deserves.

Argue all you want that the ritual of marriage has become quaint, almost fusty.

Still – not that it's any of the doubters' business – the odds of their union succeeding are quite high, thank you.

"American research suggests that remarriages made after age 40 are more stable than first marriages," StatsCan reports. "The reason dissolution risk falls as age at remarriage rises may be partly due to the partners' increased maturity."

Ah, yes, maturity. That must be it.

But I've watched my friend and her fiancé. They laugh a heck of a lot. They speak in the secret code of the love. They nurture each other, tease each other, enhance each other, annoy each other.

They have the time and inclination to focus on each other. And if they choose to honour all that in an old-fashioned, courtly manner, more power to them.

You never know. Perhaps they'll start a trend.

63 Rosa Hyphen

"Who are you? Who, who, who, who?"

— Pete Townshend of The Who (b.1945)

"A wife should no more take her husband's name than he should hers. My name is my identity and must not be lost."

— American suffragette Lucy Stone (1818-1893)

You can carbon date some couples' marriage by the fact that the female partner has a hyphenated name.

Consider: For a bride in about a six-month period in the 1970s, hyphenating was trés chic. Tying your new spouse's moniker to your own with an insouciant little slash suggested you were liberated enough to keep your identity. But in your aw-shucks-I'm-just-an-old-fashioned-girl mode, you were traditional enough to adopt the new identity bestowed on you by this thing called a husband.

OK. Maybe that wasn't you. It was *me*. I was a hyphenator.

Women stronger than I were already refusing to forfeit their birth names at marriage. No dithering for them. No vacillation. But that wasn't my nature. At the time of my first wedding over 30 years ago, I opted for a double barrel.

My then-spouse voiced no opinion about my taking his name, but I was weird enough, as far as his family was concerned. Why add to their doubts by retaining my birth name? The Harris-Adler hook-up seemed the perfect compromise. I was woman. Hear me "ahem."

It seemed like just weeks after we said our "I dos" a tipping point ensued and brides were no longer hyphenating.

Instead, they were clutching their birth names close to their hearts, badges of hard-fought independence. Still, I stood by my decision to add his name to mine. The weight of the two additional syllables was a novelty at first. The combination gave me heft and made me feel adult, substantial.

But underneath I sort of knew my choice spoke to my ambivalence. It suggested that I was neither here nor there. That little dash – the bridge between my sense of self and my sense of coupledom – was the place where I felt most comfortable. I thought of calling myself Rosa Hyphen.

Turns out, you can carbon date boomer marriage by the fact that last names were ever at issue. The wedding website The Knot says that less than 10 per cent of women hyphenate today. And while the practice of women keeping their last names, first championed by suffragette Lucy Stone in the 1850s, became a cause celébre during the feminist years of the late 20th century, the trend had peaked by the 1990s. The number has been declining ever since. Now, according to one 5,000-person survey, 82 per cent of

Canadian women are dropping their birth names to assume their husbands' surnames.

Age makes a difference. Another study showed that women who married between the ages of 35 and 39 were over six times more likely to keep their names than women who married between the ages of 20 and 24. Interestingly, however, fewer university-educated women are keeping their own names nowadays than have in the recent past.

Does this indicate a failure of the women's movement, or a feminist victory? Counter-intuitively, it's the latter, says marriage historian Stephanie Koontz. "For many women who came of age in the 1970s," she says, "it was very important symbolically for them to say 'I have my own identity. That has not disappeared just because I am married.' Now people take their separate identities for granted and don't see adopting their husbands' names as a threat," she explains.

My own hyphenated name stuck hard. As I established myself professionally, it became my byline. So when I divorced after 21 years, I faced a dilemma. Should I excise the artifact of a failed marriage?

You can carbon date some breakups, too, by the speed with which some women revert to their birth names. Maybe that was you. It wasn't me. Call it pragmatism. Call it nostalgia. Who knows why? For 11 years, I couldn't drop the appendage. Now I'm finally ready. Hear me roar.

As it happens, however, identity is a moving target. I recently learned that I wasn't always "Harris." My paternal grandfather's surname, before *he* changed it, was "Breginsky." What do I do now?

64 Dating tips for the novice

"We have so much in common. We both love soup and snow peas. We love the outdoors, and talking and not talking. We could not talk or talk forever and still find things to not talk about."

— from the movie Best in Show

"The only difference between a date and a job interview is there aren't many job interviews where there's a chance you'll end up naked at the end of it."

— Jerry Seinfeld (b: 1954)

Ah, the wonderful world of courtship – a time, presumably, when we get to talk and not talk about snow peas and soup. In some eras and cultures, this is done through the highly ritualized act of dating. If you're old enough to have dated in your 20s and 30s, that fact dates you right back. You were likely born before or during the Second World War.

By contrast, many people in the boomer age bracket are essentially virgins when it comes to this ritual. We don't know how to do it. If we've done it at all, the experience has been rare and awkward. We might have dated on occasion in high school. Proms required partners and Sweet 16 parties were less saccharine with a beau on your arm. (My poor older brother was hogtied into rounding up dates for his scrawny kid sister for both types of functions.) Even so, as the '60s bloomed, those innocent activities were already taking on a bourgeois sheen in the black-and-white thinking of the youthfully arrogant. Dating was so 1950s.

Our early adulthood made the practice seem all the more archaic, in much the same way dances with structure and steps became old fashioned. Why learn to cha-cha-cha, when you could flail your arms around with abandon? Similarly, why endure the painful process of selecting a mate by cycling through a series of boring but appropriate potentials? Why be coy? Remember: This was a time when gender roles were being thrown up in the air and landing with a thud. A handy new pill gave women freedom from pregnancy and the liberty to bed-hop. Love Potion Number Nine had to be diluted to make sure there was enough to go around. And as much as we were idealists, we were also pragmatists.

We cut – not to the chase, but away from it. We put our sexuality on the line.

Take it or leave it. Tonight or not. No harm done. No hard feelings.

Well, here we are, all these years later. Some of us are lucky enough to have found enduring romance and comfort despite the rhetoric of the era we grew up in. Others, not so much. Divorce has been epidemic among our generation – sometimes, more than one per person. "You're talking to someone who has been married to various people for the last 40 years of her life," American actor Stockard Channing once said in an interview. Then she added a telling line. "Dating is not really something familiar," she said. "I've never really been a dater."

Turns out, dating might be a useful skill after all.

These days, we are wiser, a tad more circumspect and maybe just a little less casual about whom we're prepared to get naked with, physically and metaphorically. We've spent years honing our consumer instincts by learning to be selective – but don't know how to apply those instincts to selecting a partner.

Not to worry. Your trusty Aunt Rosa has scanned the Internet in search of advice for the dating novice. Here's the best of the lot, from an unknown source.

"There are three possible parts to a date, of which at least two must be offered: entertainment, food and affection. It is customary to begin a series of dates with a great deal of entertainment, a moderate amount of food and the merest suggestion of affection. As the amount of affection increases, the entertainment can be reduced proportionately. When the affection is the entertainment, we no longer call it dating. Under no circumstances can the food be omitted."

So there you have it. Food and entertainment. Food and affection.

If, on that first outing, the affection is the entertainment, you're not really dating. You're reliving the '60s.

65 Pitching woo in the ether

"The perfect mate loves long walks on the beach, car chases on the Pacific Coast Highway, antiquing and passing out in Cadillac Escalades."

— Lindsay Lohan, in a video posted on a comedy website spoofing online dating ads

Salmon might be history. Cod might be toast. But in the Sea of Love, the fish are jumpin' and the pheromones are running high. I'm referring, here, to the Internet phenom Plenty of Fish, the free online dating service launched in 2003 by Vancouverite Markus Frind. It started with 40 members. All these years later, the site has more than 100 million registered users around the world – and counting.

In the Victoria area alone, where I live, some 1,800 souls are out there in the ether, pitching themselves like so many leaky condos in hopes of pitching woo. The men, it seems, love to dance and cook. The women are all spiritual yogis with playful sides and kayaks perched perilously atop their SmartCars.

If that sounds a tad derisive, let it be known that I've swum with the school of broken hearts and tender expectations, too. There. I said it. I'm not ashamed. Given a work environment where a wink or a casual touch can land you before a human rights tribunal, discretion isn't just valour, it's survival. And in a world where traditional venues for face-to-face flirting are on the wane – when was the last time you were at a church social? – opportunities for meeting Mr. Right Enough are limited. What's a girl to do?

What she does is hit the computer, heart beating, and pause to consider the "sensitive intellectual who likes walks on the beach, candlelit dinners and thoughtful conversation." She's not crazy about the moustache, but the rest of the face looks promising. She hopes the picture wasn't taken in 1972. She pushes a button. She waits. If she gets a response, there will be an interview in the form of a coffee date. If the stars align, there will be love.

About that "girl" thing. The woman in question hasn't been a girl since some time in 1972. Her age is on the far north of 50, but she is hardly unique. If there's any stigma still attached to online dating, you'd be hard-pressed to find it among her demographic.

Two-thirds of the Plenty-of-Fishers in the area where I live are boomers, eligible for some form of senior discount at theatres or restaurants. They're not spring chickens. They were the original guerrilla warriors of the sexual revolution. Most have been married and divorced, at least once. They are scarred, they are wounded and they are ever-optimistic. Time is short and they learn quickly to get over the initial embarrassment of marketing their souls.

Romance meets pragmatism. It all sounds so 21st-century. The truth is, of course, that matchmaking has been around, in one form or another, for just about as long as there have been human hormones. It was certainly one of the peripheral functions of the village priest or rabbi in earlier times, when Cupid took a back seat to more sensible concerns, such as the income and status of the families involved. And in cultures from the Mediterranean to the Far East, parents have always hired intermediaries to find mates for their sons and daughters, who often have little say in the choices made on their behalf. But in our stripped-down, do-it-yourself North American universe, where technology beckons and musk is pulsing through the broadband cables, many of us have opted to perform the ritual ourselves, with varying results.

True story: Mr. Moustache writes back and the "girl" finds herself sipping lattes with a man who looks vaguely familiar. They trace their roots back to a place 3,000 miles away and to another blind date. A friend had set them up. They were both 17. He was a "sensitive intellectual" even then. After several long and languorous phone conversations, he insisted it was love, demanded that they meet. She'd fancied herself in love, too. But he was a hunk. She was skinny, clumsy, tongue-tied. She feared the worst, but he persuaded her. They met for one awkward date. He never called her again.

Nearly 40 years later the bald man and the seasoned woman laugh about this unexpected reunion. Can he see her again, he asks? She gracefully declines. God knows she's mature. God knows she's sensitive, too. But she can't help feeling just a touch smug. He isn't for her. Their lives have diverged too dramatically. There's no new common ground.

She wishes him well. They part ways. She revels in the poignancy of the moment. Perhaps later, she'll jump back into the pond.

66 Flaming out

"From time to time he just makes her laugh

She cooks a meal or two

Everybody loves the sound of a train in the distance.

Everybody thinks it's true."

— Paul Simon, from the song *Train in the Distance*

You're having a casual drink with a former spouse a decade after the split-up. The rancour and fury that marked your divorce have long since dissipated. He reminds you of that time in Belize when you both tried to snorkel in two feet of water. The laugh you share feels like a warm bath. And for a moment – just a moment – you sense an odd lascivious tug in exactly the wrong direction: toward your ex.

That's the premise of *It's Complicated*, the 2009 hit movie starring Meryl Streep and Alec Baldwin. The film is a bit of fluff, really – a bedroom farce involving the kind of requisite near misses and broad emotional pratfalls that ensure boffo box office. Still and all, I suspect it struck a chord with a considerable number of people who've had that kind of hot flash with a onetime mate. Bitterness fades. Years pass. Everybody loves the sound of a train in the distance. And the farther away the train travels, the more haunting its whistle seems.

Think of it all as an enigma wrapped in nostalgia, this attraction to a partner from the past. Your instincts are in a state of flux. One part of your gut says "Go for it. What's the harm?" The other part is shouting at the top of its lungs "Danger, Will Robinson!"

What to do? Some famous couples have tried to rekindle the embers of an old flame: think Liz Taylor and Richard Burton. Their first famously stormy union – they wed in 1964 – was an exercise in smashed wine glasses, drunken recriminations and fierce, passionate verbal brawls. They called it quits ten years later, then gamely walked down the aisle again in 1975.

According to reports, an x-ray that showed spots on her lungs prompted the tempestuous Taylor to remarry the dissolute Welshman. Perhaps there's nothing like fear of the unknown to send you running straight into the arms of the comfortably familiar. All the same, the second time for them lasted a scant 10 months. No doubt, there's a lesson here.

The experts seem to think so. Gary Neuman, Oprah Winfrey's go-to rabbi, is cautious about the advisability of retracing your marital steps. "Once divorce occurs," he says, "the idea of remarriage seems daunting. If you feel that there are unresolved possibilities with your ex, go slow and explore with a lot of patience and planning."

Right. But there's that moment when you're jointly remembering your second anniversary, that bottle of Dom

Perignon, the pregnancy that resulted, the exquisite instant after the birth of your first. It's hard not to get carried away. What's more, it so happens the piano man at the bar is launching into a heartfelt version of *As Time Goes By*. The pull is strong. The lights are low. The reminiscences are flowing. The melancholy is tangible. The longing intense.

You think about the couples just like you, now celebrating their 32nd anniversary. No small accomplishment. And you wonder: why didn't we make it over the long haul? Where did we lose the way? What made us give up trying?

Marriage is a bit like being a marathon runner, you conclude. There comes a point when every muscle in your body tells you to quit. Athletes and trainers call it the burn, and the term is accurate.

You feel like you're consumed by a blazing, red-hot fire you can't escape. Some couples overcome the agony and push forward. They arrive at the finish line. You didn't. Is it time to take up the race again?

Everybody loves the sound of a train in the distance, but the truth is that when it's up close and personal, it's just noise.

Sure, there are sweet and tender moments with exes.

Certainly if you'd been then who you are now, there might have been a future for you.

But life is a moving target and we learn to mosey on.

The tug toward the sweet bygone is real. But it's also ephemeral. And that, as Martha Stewart might say, is a good thing.

67 Marie of Romania

"Oh, life is a glorious cycle of song,

A medley of extemporanea;

And love is a thing that can never go wrong;

And I am Marie of Romania."

— American writer and wit Dorothy Parker (1893-1967)

Well, polish up the tiara, good readers. Your faithful friend, here – Marie of Romania – is about to assume her eastern European nation's crown.

Which is to say your faithful friend is likely certifiable.

In what way, you ask? Consider this. After more than 10 years of singledom, she is taking a precarious plunge and moving in with a party of the opposite gender. The relationship will not be platonic – and we all know how that can turn out.

Certainly, there are those who think her recent delusions of love would best be handled with proper medication. But they're just hard-nosed cynics at worst – or fully committed to being single at best.

A lot of obviously sane people fall into the latter category. We are led to believe that there's a not-so-subtle urging imposed on all of us to find a mate. In fact, the pressure is so bad, argues American social scientist Bella DePaulo, that there's an inherent bias against those who choose to remain on their own. She calls it singleism.

Yet the trend to couple up clearly appears to be reversing. StatsCan consistently reports a truly significant increase in people living alone. In just one five-year period, for example, the number of one-person households rose by 11.8 per cent. In fact, as of 2006, more Canadian adults had never been married than had.

Queen Marie herself had been married, but her divorce a decade ago put her off the notion of a forever-after partner. The breakup shattered a dream and wounded a family. The pain was visceral and complete. As a result, she believed she was content to be single for the duration.

That didn't mean she didn't date. Men, she rediscovered, came in a fascinating, strange array of flavours. There was the Blue Suitor – a fella of great accomplishment and high rank who was bereft and depressed as retirement loomed. There was the Wild Man of the Malahat – a Hunter Thompsonesque personality who consumed all the air in the room. There was the Extreme Penny Pincher, who once requested that she find her own way home by bus at 10 o'clock on a rainy night.

While none of these oddballs diminished her desire for companionship, they also reinforced her sense of privacy and independence. She was the queen of her little castle –

and if someone left the milk out overnight, she had no one to blame except herself.

Then, along came the right guy at the right time. Marie regally resisted at first, clutching her singleness as though it were some kind of life raft. She cherished her routines. She liked being answerable to no one in particular. She enjoyed her evenings out with the girls, with no tacit curfew hanging over her head. Secretly, she feared she was too set in her ways to contemplate sharing any space with another human being.

But her gentle beau, who had learned a few things about women, was patient, sweet and reassuring. He eased each of her doubts over time – even those she didn't realize she had. He backed off when she got antsy. Cannily, he waited until this feral creature came to him. Eventually, she did.

Queen Marie remains trepidatious. What if? What if it all blows up in their faces? There could be scenes – and who needs scenes at our advanced ages? Can he deal with her family? Can she deal with his ex? Can they adapt, unbend and reinvent themselves in a shared household? Will they continue to love each other in the increasingly unforgiving light of the morning?

Turns out, the Ruler of Romania is a romantic in spite of herself. Oh yes – and as for all those single-adult households? Trust boomers to go against the grain.

Statistics Canada reports that people in their early 60s are entering into common-law relationships at the most rapid rate of all age categories.

Perhaps that's because "forever after" is far less frightening when the end of forever is on the horizon.

68 All my exes live in Texas

"Simplicity is making the journey of this life with just baggage enough."

— American journalist Charles Dudley Warner (1829 - 1900)

Everyone knows couples who married just once and have been together for 50 years. How lovely for them.

But for the rest, the world can be a Facebook nightmare of exes and exes-once-removed. Heartbreak happens. We lick our wounds and move on.

A good many of us, dreamers that we are, keep searching for our soulmates. Again. And again.

Consider the following: Ottawa's Vanier Institute of the Family reports that 26 per cent of women and 37 per cent of men "enter into a new conjugal relationship within three years of marriage dissolution." After five years, those figures jump to 36 per cent for women and 51 per cent for men. And if a first marriage has lasted 20 years, 69 per cent of women and 82 per cent of men will partner up again.

What's more, writes sociologist Ching Jiangqin Du in her thesis for the University of Western Ontario, serial cohabitation is significantly on the rise in Canada.

The fact is, if you've put a few years behind you, chances are you've put a few long-term partners behind you, too.

 This was driven home the other day when a friend casually referred to an incident that happened "a wife ago." He is now on his third. No one in the assembled group thought this at all odd.

In another recent gathering, I discovered I was a relative marriage virgin – the only one to have done the deed a single time. (I did cohabit with a Cuban bongo player for a couple of years when I was in my 20s during my exotic boyfriend phase. I am now cohabiting again – so I'm catching up, but without the bling to show for it.)

The math is boggling. Think of the infographic involved, an exponential tangle of arrows and pointers and dotted lines.

And all those exes out there are a testament to sweet folly or bitter failure, still lurking in a far distant corner of our brains and hearts.

Some exes, of course, are more significant than others. And these relationships can loom large in the minds of our new mates – especially recent couplings that consumed a good number of years.

So if they haven't met in person, our fresh partners likely have a skewed version of their earlier counterparts. They hear stories. They make judgments based on faulty information. It's inevitable.

As honest as I hope I am in conveying my ex, I've no doubt gritted my teeth a few times when spewing out his name.

Sitcom characters you never meet – think Maris, on *Frasier* – are much richer fodder for humour or derision than those who appear on the screen.

My current partner and I made a conscious decision, therefore, to meet each other's most recent ex. Was it awkward and a little intimidating? You bet. Did I calculate her weight in my head? Absolutely.

But the meeting also demystified her and turned her into a human being.

As for my partner, my meeting his ex represented a kind of (so sorry for the term) closure that served to normalize us as a couple. If she's going to be a part of his life – and she always will be, in some capacity – it's important for all of us that I can put a face to a name.

As we transition to new partners, we have a choice. We can keep significant exes siloed and removed, or we can gingerly incorporate them into our doings. They don't – and shouldn't – take up residence in our back pockets. But they deserve a place in the landscape of our lives all the same.

It's a show of respect for all parties involved and a reflection of our willingness to let the past go. I know the next time I meet her, for instance, I won't feel the need to size her up. She will just be a fact.

Baggage is us – but how much we end up carrying is a personal choice.

69 I do

"The secret of a happy marriage remains a secret."

— Comedian Henny Youngman (1906 - 1998)

"Marriage is a strange combination of dream and reality, and we spend our lives as couples trying to negotiate that divide."

— Writer Elizabeth Gilbert (b: 1969)

We are lying under the blankets on a blustery night in late winter. Decay and rebirth are duking it out like clashing lovers in a driving rainstorm beyond our window. Here in our bedroom, though, we're feeling snug and warm in every possible way.

Our wide-ranging conversation – one of the three things we fully enjoy together in this sanctuary – has reached a lull. (The third is listening to music. We've shut that off, too.)

Right now, as I start to drift, a feeling hearkens back to childhood – a mood experienced so long ago that I can't quite put a name to it, although carefree comes closest.

Slumber is within easy reach. Then, a mumble in the dark. The mood is shattered.

"What do you think," says the pragmatist beside me, and I am suddenly alert to a tentative quality in his voice. "Maybe if we're still together in five years – maybe we should, I dunno, consider getting married."

I'm gob-smacked. So much for sleep. He's used the "m" word, no matter that he's talking half a decade down the road. I should have known. Things have been going far too well. I love the man deeply – no question – but we have three failed marriages between us. Surely the enterprise of matrimony is a curse on long-term happiness.

The room becomes dead still. No clock ticks ominously, second-hand ever louder, on the bedside table: who owns a wind-up these days? But some foreboding sound should mark the occasion. My immediate unspoken reaction: "Why?"

I don't have to mouth the word. Sensing his dear in the headlights, he makes his argument. He says people see couples in a different way when they're married – take them more seriously. He wants to present that face to the world – to show it that we mean business and that ours is no fly-by-night affair. (He knows better than to say *like all the others you've had.*)

I hold my tongue and search for some inanity to get me through this seriously strange moment. Where did this come from? He knows my history. When he and I met I'd been living on my own for a decent portion of my adult life, dating happily, coming home to the privacy and comfort of my own little lair. Defiantly independent. Contentedly single. Plucky, even.

Moving in with him had been a big enough step for me and, yes – touch wood – it has gone wildly better than either of us expected.

I haven't subsumed myself in him. I didn't "immediately vanish into [his] … chest cavity like a twisted, unrecognizable, parasitical homunculus," as Elizabeth Gilbert writes of her once primal fear of commitment. Nor has he become reliant, infantile or demanding – my own worst nightmare.

For two terrific years, we've been thoroughly adult – effortlessly loving, respectful, autonomous – and we have each other's back in a big way. Still, the arrangement feels provisional, somehow: we continue to walk on eggs that exist only in our fearful imaginations. We have yet to fight. When we finally do, what if it's a whopper? I haven't lost my skittishness. And just the other day he told the gang at the local that he'd never be doing *that* again.

How to react? "It's a thought," I say, to buy time, and am astonished to find the idea actually taking shape in my brain. I unfold it there like it's a clothing item in a boutique I never frequent. I try it on for size. To my amazement, the fit is perfect. But does it suit me? I fiddle around until it clings to me just so.

Another shock: it looks good, really good. Age appropriate? Can't say. But very sexy. The cost is unfathomable and the return policy is harsh. If I take it, will there be buyer's remorse?

"Why?" I finally ask, reasonably. I intend to add *Why jinx a great thing*, but my mouth betrays me. Instead, out comes "Why wait five years?"

"You're right," he replies. "Why wait?" I sense his smile in the dark. Is it sly?

He takes prenuptial rituals seriously. We aren't engaged, he insists, until he presents me with a ring. That might take weeks.

Here is my opportunity to back down, to retreat. I give myself room to let that happen, but it doesn't. Almost in spite of myself, I'm greeting the prospect of our combined future with quiet, sure-footed confidence.

Divorce statistics be damned. The odds against us finding the One Big Romance, especially at this late stage of life, are far greater. Yet here we are. Call it the triumph of rebirth over decay. And it really doesn't matter how many times you get the institution wrong. Alchemy happens when love is sanctioned by the tribe.

The ring has surprising significance. He presents it to me with ceremony and I formally accept his proposal.

Just over a month later, at our elopement, the marriage commissioner concludes the brief service with a hearty *Mazel Tov* pronounced in her thick, Scottish brogue.

We are giddy. We are exhilarated. What have we done? Oh my, what have we done?

Emphasis on *we*. Emphasis on *we*, forever.

About the Author

Writer and editor Rosa Harris is a two-time Canadian National Magazine Award winner.

She has penned stories for many major North American publications on topics ranging from baby food to global economics.

Rosa was editor of *Ottawa City* magazine for nearly a decade. As well, she has served as a judge for both the National Magazine Awards and the National Newspaper Awards in Canada, has been a newspaper columnist for *The Ottawa Citizen* and *The Victoria Times Colonist*, has taught journalism at four universities and occasionally serves as a talk show host.

Rosa resides, happily, in Victoria, BC.

Boomerville is her first published book.

Manor House
905-648-2193